AF255723

"From the introduction which points us to a deeper reverence and understanding of the Lord's Supper and the significance that it holds, this book offers pastors and lay leaders alike a useful resource for ministry. *Come to the Table* contains a variety of excellent stories and illustrations that are tied to the calendar year that could easily be used to impact church worship around the practice of communion."

—BARRY LIND, senior pastor, Northwood Christian Church

"When I prepare thoughts for the Lord's Supper, I'm always looking for a good thought, a biblical insight, and a fresh idea. Thanks to Knox and Heine, I now have sixty new meditations. If you are needing help preparing an introduction to the Lord's Supper or just want a book to help you find the heart of our faith, *Come to the Table* is the resource for you."

—MILTON JONES, president, Christian Relief Fund

"Knox and Heine, with scholarly minds and pastoral hearts, offer every elder, deacon, congregational member, and gospel minister who presides over the Lord's table sixty concise and Christ-saturated devotional reflections on our king's meal. *Come to the Table* is a needed resource which blends beautiful and thoughtful stories from everyday life, from authors like Henri Nouwen, from the apostolic fathers, and from mature reflection, each set alongside wisely chosen biblical passages. What a gift."

—J. K. JONES, Lincoln Christian University

"In every family, coming to the table helps form identity in community. For followers of Jesus, the family table is communion. This book is a gift to the church. It is both deep in history and tradition, yet also current and applicable to the life of faith today. The powerfully grounding introduction and the sixty Christ-centered meditations all invite us to joyfully and humbly come to the table and feast!"

—Tim Knight, pastor, Highline Christian Church

Come to the Table

Come to the Table

Meditations on the Lord's Supper

GEORGE M. KNOX

RONALD E. HEINE

CASCADE *Books* · Eugene, Oregon

COME TO THE TABLE
Meditations on the Lord's Supper

Copyright © 2023 Wipf and Stock. All rights reserved. Except for brief
quotations in critical publications or reviews, no part of this book may
be reproduced in any manner without prior written permission from the
publisher. Write: Permissions, Wipf and Stock Publishers, 199 W. 8th Ave.,
Suite 3, Eugene, OR 97401.

Cascade Books
An Imprint of Wipf and Stock Publishers
199 W. 8th Ave., Suite 3
Eugene, OR 97401

www.wipfandstock.com

PAPERBACK ISBN: 978-1-6667-5243-4
HARDCOVER ISBN: 978-1-6667-5244-1
EBOOK ISBN: 978-1-6667-5245-8

Cataloguing-in-Publication data:

Names: Knox, George M., author. | Heine, Ronald E., author.

Title: Come to the table : meditations on the Lord's Supper / George M.
Knox and Ronald E. Heine.

Description: Eugene, OR: Cascade Books, 2023 | Includes
bibliographical references.

Identifiers: ISBN 978-1-6667-5243-4 (paperback) | ISBN 978-1-6667-
5244-1 (hardcover) | ISBN 978-1-6667-5245-8 (ebook)

Subjects: LCSH: Lord's Supper. | Meditations.

Classification: BV825.3 C55 2023 (paperback) | BV825.3 (ebook)

07/21/23

To our wives,
Frances and Gillian

Contents

ADVENT & CHRISTMAS

LENT, EASTER, & PENTECOST

Permissions

Note-Takers Bible, New American Standard Updated Edition. Copyright 1999 by the Lockman Foundation. All Rights Reserved. Copyright 1960, 1962, 1963, 1968, 1971, 1972, 1973, 1975, 1977, 1995 by the Lockman Foundation.

The Holy Bible, New International Version. Copyright 1978 by New York International Bible Society.

The Christian Life Bible. Copyright 1985, by Porter L. Barrington. The Holy Bible, New King James Version. Copyright 1985 by Thomas Nelson, Inc.

Holy Bible, New Living Translation, copyright 1996, 2004, 2007 by Tyndale House Foundation. All rights reserved. Scripture quotations marked NLT are taken from the Holy Bible, New Living Translation, copyright 1996, 2004, 2007 by Tyndale House Foundation. Used by permission of Tyndale House Publishers, Inc., Carol Stream, Illinois 60188. All rights reserved.

NRSV New Revised Standard Version Bible. Copyright 1989 by the Division of Christian Education of the National Council of the Churches of Christ in the United States of America.

Preface

The Christian observance of the Lord's Supper has its roots in the last meal that Jesus shared with his disciples on the night before his crucifixion. In the course of that meal Jesus "took a loaf of bread, and after blessing it he broke it, gave it to them, and said, 'Take; this is my body.' Then he took a cup, and after giving thanks he gave it to them, and all of them drank from it. He said to them, 'This is my blood of the covenant, which is poured out for many'" (Mark 14:22–24, NRSV). From the earliest days of the church down to the present Christians have made the observance of the Lord's Supper a central part of worship.

One of the customs that has grown up around this practice in some Christian traditions is to have a short meditation related to the Lord's Supper prior to its observance. Sometimes these are given by the pastor, and sometimes they are given by a layperson who is presiding at the table of the Lord. For several years George Knox and I attended a small congregation of Christians that met in a church building located in a valley surrounded by the forest-covered hills just outside Eugene, Oregon. We were part of a group of several members of this congregation who gave meditations prior to the participation in the Lord's Supper. We have culled out some of our meditations for this book in the hope that they may be useful for laypeople who perform this service in other congregations. We also hope that they may be useful for some as private meditations on the essential events of the Christian faith that are central to the Lord's Supper.

R. H.

Maundy Thursday, 2022

Abbreviations

FOTC	Fathers of the Church
NAS	New American Standard
NIV	New International Version
NKJV	New King James Version
NLT	New Living Translation
NRSV	New Revised Standard Version

Introduction

George M. Knox

For twenty centuries the Lord's Supper has played a major role in the life of the church. The form and frequency have varied while the primary focus has remained the same. It has been observed as frequently as daily and as seldom as yearly. In the beginning it was part of a meal called the "love (*agape*) feast." As time passed the love feast was replaced by a carefully structured liturgy of prayers, homily, and Scripture for its observance. In some parts of the church more changes in form and frequency occurred as many Christians sought a simpler, unadorned service. While the Lord's Supper has almost always been observed in a church sanctuary of some kind, the earliest record of it in the New Testament indicates it took place in house churches. A group setting is most common but sometimes a forced isolation has made it an individual affair. Russell Morse, a Christian missionary, was held prisoner in a Chinese Communist jail prior to World War II. He saved back a tiny portion of his meager rice meal and water and used them for a private communion each day. Recently the COVID-19 virus led to social distancing and lockdowns. For a time, churches stopped having in-person meetings. Instead, people worshiped in the privacy of their homes, using whatever they had on hand for the communion elements. From the beginning wine has been one of the elements used to represent the blood of Christ, but in some cases, this has not been possible. For example, a missionary in a remote part of Ethiopia, where no grapes were available, used Kool-Aid.

Jesus gave no instructions about form and frequency of this observance. In the tradition handed on by Paul, written before any of the Gospels, Jesus said, "Do this in remembrance of me" (1 Cor 11:24 NRSV). He also said, "as often as you do this," implying that he expected it to be a regular occurrence. Many things about the observance of the Lord's Supper have changed but one constant remains. It has been and always will be all about Jesus Christ and the good news of what he has done, is doing, and will yet do on our behalf. In short, the Lord's Supper in action and symbol summarizes the Gospel.

THE LORD'S SUPPER AS "GOSPEL"

A student at a Christian college never failed to ask his professor the same question about that day's chapel sermon: "Was that Gospel or Law?" He was a little older than the usual college student and had been raised in the tradition of a Midwest Reformed church. For him, the sermon was either "Law" or "Gospel." It is not unusual for the sermon to focus on moral, ethical, or lifestyle issues. Such sermons are perfectly good biblical sermons, but they are not "gospel." Paul defined the gospel in 1 Corinthians 15. The "good news" (gospel) he preached was: "that Christ died for our sins in accordance with the scriptures, and that he was buried, and that he was raised on the third day in accordance with the scriptures, and that he appeared to Cephas, then to the twelve. Then he appeared to more than five hundred brothers and sisters at one time, most of whom are still alive, though some have died. Then he appeared to James, then to all the apostles. Last of all, as to one untimely born, he appeared also to me" (1 Cor 15:3–8 NRSV). The good news is centered in Jesus Christ himself: his death, burial, resurrection, and the fact that he is alive. This is exactly what the Lord's Supper is focused on. Wherever, and whenever, a church presents the Eucharist, the gospel is proclaimed.

It is not surprising, therefore, that the Lord's Supper has been an essential part of the church's life for twenty centuries. Some have compared it to a brilliant, sparkling diamond. It has been said "diamonds are forever." Our culture prizes them and is willing to pay huge sums to get them. What gives them their value and lasting beauty? A natural diamond dug out of the earth is not brilliant and beautiful. The sparkle and brilliance depend on how it is cut and polished. It takes a master craftsman to bring out its beauty. Most brilliant cut diamonds have about fifty-eight triangle and kite-shaped facets. Light enters the diamond and strikes one facet of the stone and then another, giving the stone its sparkle. The Lord's Supper was given to us by a master craftsman and like a diamond it has many facets. Each of these facets connects us to Christ and to his body, the church. Each has its biblical story and leads us to many themes for study and meditation. Following are some of the facets that give the Eucharist its beauty.

"WHEN HE HAD GIVEN THANKS"—EUCHARIST

Thanksgiving is a prominent theme in all the Lord's Supper narratives. Consequently, the service has been known from early Christian times as the "Thanksgiving" (*eucharistia* in Greek). In its very essence the Lord's Supper is a response of thanksgiving to the grace of God. At the Last Supper Jesus undoubtedly said the prayers commonly used in the Passover meal. Such prayers did not ask God to bless the food. Rather they blessed, or thanked God, who had given freedom. Likewise, in the Lord's Supper the whole church gives thanks to God for his gracious acts in Jesus Christ. Paul wrote in 2 Corinthians 4:15 (NRSV), "Everything is for your sake, so that grace, as it extends to more and more people, may increase thanksgiving to the glory of God."

The Didache, a late-first- or early-second-century document, provides a prayer for giving thanks at the Eucharist: "Concerning the Eucharist, give thanks as follows: First, concerning the cup, We give you thanks, our Father, for the holy vine of David your servant, which you have made known to us through Jesus, your servant; to you be the glory forever. And, concerning the broken bread, We give you thanks, our Father, for the life and knowledge, that you made known to us through Jesus, your servant; to you be the glory forever."[1]

SHARING—*KOINONIA*

Paul uses the term *koinonia* in 1 Corinthians 10:16–17 (NRSV) to indicate the meaning of our action in taking communion. He speaks of it as a twofold sharing: "The cup of blessing that we bless, is it not a sharing in the blood of Christ? The bread that we break, is it not a sharing in the body of Christ? Because there is one bread, we who are many are one body, for we all partake of the one bread." In communion we share in the blood and body of Christ. *Koinonia* appears in various Bible translations as "fellowship," "communion," "sharing," and "participation." The latter term includes the idea of investing oneself in the life and cause of another person.

When Paul speaks about sharing in the blood of Christ, he undoubtedly has in mind the words of Jesus that he quotes in 1 Corinthians 11:25 (NRSV), "This cup is the new covenant in my blood" (see also Luke 22:20). Mark and Matthew use the phrase, "the blood of the covenant" (Mark 14:24; Matt 26:28). Alan Richardson comments: "The words of Jesus at the Last Supper as recorded by St Mark are a clear reference to Exodus 24:8.[2] These words echo what Moses said at the covenant making on Sinai. After reading the book of the covenant to the people, and they had promised to obey all that he had read, Moses took the blood of sacrificed animals and dashed it on the people, and said, 'See the blood of the covenant that the Lord has made with you in accordance with all these words.' Jesus was saying that his death 'was the sacrificial act by which God was making a covenant with a new people, replacing the old, broken Covenant of Sinai.'"[3]

1. *Didache* 9.1–3, in Holmes, *Apostolic Fathers*, 357, 359.
2. Richardson, *Introduction*, 230.
3. Richardson, *Introduction*, 231.

Jesus was asking his disciples for commitment. He was asking them to enter a partnership, a sharing in a new covenant. Paul makes this clear when he compares three types of meals. One is the Lord's Supper in 1 Corinthians 10:16–17. The second type is Jewish meals where the sacrifice is eaten (v. 18), and third are the meals at the table of a pagan god (vv. 19–21). Richard Hays comments, "[W]hat they have in common is this: Each meal creates a relation of *koinonia* ('fellowship') among the participants and between the participants and the deity honored in the meal." Consequently, Paul's argument is that "The God who demands exclusive allegiance will not tolerate cultic eating that establishes a bond with any other gods or powers."[4]

The partnership Jesus calls for is also with one another in the body of Christ. As noted above, Paul wrote about this in 1 Corinthians 10:16–17, where he indicated that partaking of the one bread is sharing in the body of Christ. The phrase, "a sharing in the body of Christ," can be taken in two ways. It can refer to how, by faith and in some mysterious way, we participate with Christ in his death. Paul seems to say this in Galatians 2:20 (NRSV): "I have been crucified with Christ; and it is no longer I who live, but it is Christ who lives in me. And the life I now live in the flesh I live by faith in the Son of God, who loved me and gave himself for me."

"Sharing in the body of Christ" also means being part of a covenant community, the church, where the commitment is to one another. Ben Witherington's comments on *koinonia* are helpful:

> The translation of the word as "common participation" gets across the idea that it is a group activity. It is something worshipers do together. What believers are sharing in is not just one another but some third thing to which the word *koinonia* refers. The translation "fellowship" is not helpful, though fellowship is presumably one of the results of believers sharing or participating in something in common. . . . There seems to be some real, spiritual communion with Christ and others at issue here. Perhaps

4. Hays, *First Corinthians*, 167.

Paul is thinking of the sharing of the benefits of Christ's death—cleansing, forgiveness, salvation.[5]

There is mystery in all of this. The communion provides an opportunity for a close encounter with Jesus. He comes to meet us, and we are invited to "taste and see that the Lord is good" (Ps 34:8). By faith we experience the spiritual presence of Jesus Christ; we share in his body and blood.

ANTICIPATION—HOPE
"UNTIL HE COMES"

Just as the Passover meal looked back to deliverance from bondage in Egypt and forward to a coming Messiah, so the Lord's Supper looks back to deliverance from bondage to sin and forward to the messianic banquet. Jesus himself expressed this forward-looking view when he instituted the Lord's Supper. Twice in Luke 22:15–18 Jesus spoke of what he anticipated. Fred Craddock comments: "The Passover was very forward-looking, the food to be eaten after the family had packed their belongings for the journey to the promised land. So here the words of Jesus probably point forward to the messianic banquet, although his words have an interim fulfillment in the post-resurrection meals with the disciples (Luke 24:30–31, 41–42; Acts 1:4; 10:41)."[6] Luke's version of the Last Supper adds a third reference to eating and drinking with Jesus in the kingdom. It comes when Jesus intervenes in a dispute among the disciples as to who should be considered the greatest among them. He points out that the father conferred on him a kingdom and he will do the same for them "so that you may eat and drink at my table in the kingdom" (22:24–30 NRSV).

Paul recognized the hope found in the Lord's Supper. After reminding the Corinthians of the tradition he had shared with them, he added, "As often as you eat this bread and drink the cup, you proclaim the Lord's death until he comes" (1 Cor 11:26 NRSV). The Lord's Supper is a visible sermon, and each participant is a silent

5. Witherington, *Making a Meal*, 44–45.
6. Craddock, *Luke*, 256.

preacher proclaiming the gospel for all to see. The Lord's Supper is not just a remembrance. It is a proclamation that brings the past into the present by offering the good news of forgiveness from the crucified Christ and, at the same time, looks to the future consummation of the kingdom when the Lord returns.

This facet of the Lord's Supper invites joyful anticipation and celebration, but it can also become a problem. Both parts of his statement were necessary. The Lord's Supper was a proclamation of both the Lord's death and of his coming. In celebrating the future coming of the Lord, Paul did not want the Corinthians to forget that it was the Lord's death that they proclaimed. It seems that their celebration had become excessive. Some of the Corinthians, probably the more affluent, were celebrating by eating and drinking too much while ignoring their less fortunate members. The result was a divided church. The commitment to one another in the covenant community was shattered. Moreover, their behavior abused the Lord's Supper so that the meal was not in fact the Lord's Supper (1 Cor 11:19–20). What the world saw was not the good news of Jesus' death, resurrection, and coming again, but the bad news of a church divided.

At its best the church breaks bread and pours the cup to anticipate the great messianic banquet that is coming. We follow the example of the early church, which believed strongly in the ongoing establishment of the kingdom of God, that it was both present and coming. Wherever God's sovereignty is recognized and his will is done, the kingdom is present. But it is far from complete—it is still coming. When the Lord has returned, and the kingdom is fully established, all will gather at the table of the Lord. There will be no more Jew or Greek . . . (Gal 3:23), no hunger or thirst, and every tear will be wiped away (Rev 7:15–17). A eucharistic prayer used first in the Catholic Mass but now used also in many churches says it well:

> Christ has died. Christ is risen. Christ will come again.
> Dying, you destroyed our death. Rising you restored our life.
> Lord Jesus come in glory.
> When we eat this bread and drink this cup, we proclaim
> your death,
> Until you come in glory.

Lord, by your cross and resurrection, you have set us free.
You are the Savior of the world.

REMEMBERING JESUS: IN THE BEGINNING

In the upper room, when Jesus met with his apostles for the Passover meal, after giving them the bread and cup he said, "Do this in remembrance of me" (1 Cor 11:24 NRSV). When the church began on Pentecost, with Peter and the other apostles leading, it was not long before they met together and remembered Jesus in the "breaking of bread." Luke tells us this in his first summary statement about the infant church: "They devoted themselves to the apostles' teaching and fellowship, to the breaking of bread and the prayers" (Acts 2:42 NRSV). Luke also uses the phrase "breaking of bread" in his story of the two men of Emmaus who recognized Jesus in "the breaking of the bread" (Luke 24:35 NRSV). The Synoptic Gospels also show Jesus breaking bread and giving it to his apostles to distribute among the people in the stories of feeding the five thousand and the four thousand (Matt 14:19; 15:36; Mark 6:41; 8:6; Luke 9:16). These descriptions foreshadow the action of Jesus at the Last Supper.

What would the apostles who provided the teaching and set the direction and tone for the Lord's Supper have remembered about Jesus? There are many possibilities, of course, but it seems reasonable to think that uppermost in their minds would have been the most recent memories, starting with the Last Supper in the upper room and the events immediately prior to and following the meal. Second, and the most recent, would be their experiences with Jesus between the resurrection and Pentecost. Both sets of experiences were accompanied by powerful emotions that would have made the memories stronger.

If their remembering had been limited to their experience in the upper room, along with connected events, both prior and after the Last Supper, it would not have been a joyful experience. With some variations, the Synoptic Gospels agree on the sequence of events that must have created painful memories. The *New Interpreter's Study Bible* comments: "The text instituting the ritual of the Lord's Supper or Eucharist is surrounded by stories recounting the disciples upcoming failures, providing a somber context for Jesus' words."[7] Among their memories would be these incidents:

- Jesus, not for the first time, predicts his death: "You know that after two days the Passover is coming, and the Son of Man will be handed over to be crucified" (Matt 26:2 NRSV).

- A plot to kill Jesus, the betrayal by Judas, and the anointing at Bethany also set the tone. The disciples may not have known about some of this at the time, but the impression is that the atmosphere was filled with portents of Jesus' coming death (Mark 14:1–9).

- Near the beginning of the meal, according to Luke, Jesus said, "I have eagerly desired to eat this Passover with you *before I suffer*" (Luke 22:15 NRSV, my emphasis).

- With the Twelve at the table Jesus predicted that one would betray him. They were distressed and one after another said, "Surely, not I" (Mark 14:17–19 NRSV).

- When Jesus referred to the bread as his body and the cup of the new covenant as his blood it must have puzzled and shocked the disciples. It was certainly not Passover language.

- At the end of the meal Jesus predicted that all of them would desert him and that Peter would deny him (Mark 14:26–31).

After singing a psalm, they went to Gethsemane, Jesus was arrested, and finally crucified. And, as Jesus predicted, the Twelve deserted him. These would have been sad, even overwhelming memories for the apostles. But they did not deny or forget them. In the breaking of the bread, they remembered what he suffered and what that suffering had come to mean to them. These stories have been handed on to us and it is appropriate, even essential, that they be shared in our communion meditations. But the story doesn't end there.

7. *The New Interpreter's Study Bible*, 1837.

The "Last Supper" was actually not the last meal the disciples had with Jesus. After the resurrection there were several more. Peter's words to Cornelius in Acts 10:39–41 indicate how important these meals were to them. When Peter described the gospel that he preached he included the fact that he and other witnesses "ate and drank with him after he rose from the dead" (Acts 10:41 NRSV). Acts 1:4 offers further evidence that Jesus ate regularly with his disciples after the resurrection. The NRSV says: "While staying with them . . ." Other versions also say "staying with them," or "gathering them," which is one way to translate the Greek word used by Luke. However, the word *sunalizomenos,* means literally, "to eat salt with," or "to eat with."[8] The NRSV and other versions have a footnote indicating the translation could be "while eating with them."

Two of those meals are described by Luke. One is in the story of the two men of Emmaus who met a stranger as they sadly made their way from Jerusalem to their home. The stranger's identity was hidden from them as he explained the Scriptures about the Messiah and his death. When they arrived at Emmaus, they urged him to stay with them since the day was almost over. Then Luke says, "When he was at table with them, he took bread, blessed, and broke it, and gave it to them. Then their eyes were opened, and they recognized him" (Luke 24:30–31 NRSV). The second meal scene takes place when the two men hurry back to Jerusalem and tell the eleven apostles that Jesus was made known to them in the breaking of the bread. As they told their story, Jesus appeared among them and, Luke says, "While in their joy they were disbelieving and still wondering, he said to them, 'Have you anything here to eat?' They gave him a piece of broiled fish and he took it and ate it in their presence" (Luke 24:41–43 NRSV). The reality of his presence gave them joy.

Other meals with the resurrected Jesus are mentioned in John 21:12 and possibly in Mark 16:14 (in the disputed ending). Oscar Cullmann argues that the post-resurrection meals that Jesus shared with the disciples would have added another dimension to the

8. Rienecker, *Linguistic Key,* 263.

observance of the Lord's Supper. He says, "The certainty of the resurrection was the essential motive of the primitive Lord's Supper."[9]

As the early church met for teaching, fellowship, and prayer, Jesus' followers also "devoted themselves to the breaking of bread" (Acts 2:42 NRSV). There must have been joy at the table. Jesus was alive. They would not have forgotten about that painful time that included the Last Supper, but uppermost in the minds of the apostles would have been their experience with the post-resurrection Jesus. They, and the church with them, would have been joyfully aware of a risen Christ.

The brilliant, sparkling gem we call "the Lord's Supper" was given to us by a master craftsman. From it shines forth the gospel of salvation, which evokes thanksgiving. It unites us with Christ in his death and draws us together as his disciples into a love (*agape*) relationship. The communion also lifts our vision to the future and the glorious celebration when the kingdom is consummated. At the same time, it focuses on Jesus Christ, helping us to remember who he was, what he has done for us and will yet do. These are a few of the facets, or planes of meaning, that make the Lord's Supper a shining, brilliant thing of value and beauty. Other facets can be seen in the larger narratives of the Gospels and Epistles, including the book of Revelation, such as, atonement, peace, self-examination, repentance, forgiveness, grace, and others, all of which speak to the needs, hopes, and routines of daily life.

9. Cullmann and Leenhardt, *Essays*, 12.

Ordinary Time

I

Ordinary Time (RH)

The church calendar in the Revised Common Lectionary, which is followed by a majority of mainline churches, is divided into two kinds of time. Some blocks of time are designated by a special event in the life of Christ and the church, such as Advent, which designates the period leading up to the celebration of the birth of Christ; or Lent, which is the name given to the weeks leading up to the crucifixion and resurrection of Jesus. That is followed immediately by the period leading up to Pentecost, when the Holy Spirit was poured out on the church. Then after Pentecost there are no more specially designated periods of time in the Christian year until the next Advent season. This stretch of undesignated time makes up the larger period of time in the year. This period of time is often given the title in the Christian calendar of "Ordinary Time." It does not mean dull or unattractive, as the term "ordinary" is sometimes used in our common speech. It just means that there is no special event in the life of Christ or the church that is being anticipated in this period of time.

The larger portion of the Christian year consists of "ordinary time." That is appropriate, I think. It corresponds with how life works. The bigger part of our lives consists of ordinary time—nothing special, just the normal activities that make up everyday life. Every life, of course, also has its big, special events. Some of you have experienced new additions to your families in the last few months or weeks. That's not ordinary time! And you will celebrate those birthdays in the years to come as special days. But then you will go back to your normal routine in ordinary life. Hopefully that will not be boring, but it will lack that excitement and anticipation that led up to the birth itself.

Our Christian lives, too, are lived primarily in ordinary time. Nothing particularly eye-opening happens to us or for us as we try to follow Jesus day after day. But each Sunday when we participate in the Lord's Supper we are, for a brief moment at least, snatched out of ordinary time and thrust into the presence of Christ himself as we hear him say, "Take, eat; this is my body," and when we lift the cup to our lips he says, "Drink from it, all of you; for this is my blood of the covenant, which is poured out for many for the forgiveness of sins" (Matt 26:26–28 NRSV).

2

Binding the Strong Man (RH)

There is a children's story that I used to read to our daughter when she was small. It comes from the ancient Greek fables of Aesop. It is about a meeting of a group of mice to discuss what to do about the terror that the household cat holds over them. They make several suggestions, but one immediately pleases them. It is the cat's stealth that makes him so dangerous to the mice. They never know when he is near, until he pounces. If there was a bell on the cat, then they would know where the cat was at all times. They are in agreement that what they must do is put a bell on the cat, then the advantage of stealth will be removed. All the mice are happy because they have come up with a solution to their problem, until one skeptical old mouse in the back of the room stands up and asks, "And who is going to tie the bell around the cat's neck?" The mice did not discuss that solution anymore.

Jesus tells a short story with a similar point in Mark 3:27 (NRSV). "No one," he says, "can enter a strong man's house and plunder his property without first tying up the strong man; then indeed the house can be plundered."

This saying is set in the context of a conflict with the scribes from Jerusalem, who accused Jesus of being in league with Beelzebul, whom they called "the ruler of the demons" (Mark 3:22). The controversy had its basis in the fact that Jesus had been casting out demons. The scribes accused him of being in league with Beelzebul or Satan, who is the ruler of the demons. The demons belong to Satan. Jesus points out to them that that cannot be true. If I am in league with Satan, he says, then Satan is fighting against himself. Satan is casting out Satan. This would mean that Satan is working for his own downfall. But that is ridiculous. No one fights against himself for his own destruction.

There must, then, be another explanation. And that other explanation is what Jesus offers in the short story about the strong man. Satan is the strong man, but Jesus is clearly plundering his property by casting out demons. He could not do this unless he had first bound the strong man. That means, of course, that he is more powerful than the strong man, and has overcome him.

In this short story about binding the strong man Jesus announces his victory over Satan. This is not something that we talk about much today. One rarely hears Satan or the demonic mentioned in a church service, or the victory of Christ over the demonic forces of the world. You are more likely to hear about demons in a movie theater than in a church. But this subject looms large in the New Testament and in the thought of the early church.

Jesus came into this world to do battle with Satan, and to deliver humanity from his hold. This is what this short saying is talking about in the binding of the strong man and the plundering of his property. The property of Satan that is being plundered is humanity. The demons being cast out are not the property that is being snatched from Satan. They are Satan's allies. The property that is being plundered from Satan's house are the people who have been under Satan's control, but whom Jesus has set free.

One of the early Christian explanations of what Jesus accomplished on the cross was that he there defeated Satan. The crucifixion and resurrection of Jesus were understood as a divine conflict between Christ and Satan, and Christ was the victor. John makes this more explicit than the other Gospels. At the last meal Jesus eats with his disciples, he takes a piece of bread, dips it, and gives it to Judas. John comments, "After he [Judas] received the piece of bread, *Satan entered into him.* Jesus said to him, 'Do quickly what you are going to do'" (John 13:27 NRSV, my emphasis). The big, final, decisive battle was about to begin. And when it was over, Jesus had won.

3

A Place to Come Back To (GK)

When he was chancellor of Emmanuel Christian Seminary, Dr. Bob Wetzel wrote in the seminary's newsletter about the decision he and his wife Bonnie made several years ago to be cremated upon their deaths. When they told their girls it resulted in a lot of conversation. The first obvious question the girls asked was, "What shall we do with the ashes?" He wrote, "You would have to understand our family to appreciate the macabre humor that followed. One possibility was to throw them off the bank in the woods near our home of almost fifty years. Or the ashes could be taken back to the home of our youth in western Kansas to let the prevailing southwest wind blow them as part of a typical dust storm."

He added: "The humor continued with even more ridiculous possibilities for 'waste management.' But then our older daughter became serious and said, 'No, we need a place to come back to.'" Then Bob said, "I thought of how I always visited my parents' grave whenever we visited western Kansas. Nearby is the grave of our son who died in infancy. Yes, I had a place to come back to, to remember, and somehow say to them, 'You are remembered and loved.'"

After Jesus died, they put him in a borrowed tomb. It became for a couple of days "the place to come back to." And several disciples went there—but it was empty. Since then, disciples can go to the "tomb" in the Church of the Holy Sepulcher, but he isn't there either. Or they can go to the beautiful Garden of the Tomb in

Jerusalem and, while it feels more authentic, it too does not qualify as "the place to come back to."

Jesus must have known that his disciples would need a place to come back to—a place that actually exists; a place that is tangible and real; a place that every disciple knows about and knows exactly where it is; a place where our Lord is present. This could well be one of the reasons for giving us the Lord's Supper. It certainly serves this purpose. Frances and I have taken communion thousands of times in our home churches. We have also taken it in a Wisconsin Lutheran Church, a cathedral in England, among the ruins of ancient Corinth, and in many other places. But wherever the Lord's Supper is observed it is the place to come back to, to remember, and somehow say to our Lord, "You are remembered and loved."

4

A Table in the Wilderness (GK)

I sat in the living room early on a quiet morning with a cup of tea, and looked out upon a tranquil neighborhood bathed in bright sunshine and thought, "It appears that all is well." But looks can be deceptive. I had also just picked up the morning paper. It told a different story—a story of over one-half million deaths from CO-VID-19, of thousands who had lost their jobs, a murderer killed by the police in a standoff, a governor accused of sexual assault, and a cover-up of COVID-19 deaths. There were also threats of domestic terrorism, political deadlock, a pending ecological disaster, and protestors being gassed. You get the idea. It's a jungle, a wild wilderness out there, and we must travel through it.

It's enough to make us question God. Israel certainly did. They were in the wilderness of Sinai, weary, frightened, hungry, and thirsty. In their desperation, says Psalm 78:19 (NRSV), "They spoke against God, saying, 'Can God spread a table in the wilderness?'" They were asking, can God give us the nourishment we need to survive in this environment? Can God really produce a sense of hope and promise in the midst of such a depressing, mind-boggling situation?

Yes, said the psalmist, he can, and he did. Psalm 78 reviews Israel's history in the wilderness and asserts: "He commanded the skies above and opened the doors of heaven; he rained down on them manna to eat and gave them the grain of heaven. Mortals ate the bread of the angels; he sent them food in abundance" (Ps 78:23–25 NRSV).

Can God spread a table in our wilderness? John's story in chapter 6 says he can. A few days after feeding the five thousand in a "secluded" and "desolate" place (Mark 6:32, 35 NAS), Jesus was found again, as John tells us, by a large crowd (John 6:25). When some, seeking more bread, spoke of Israel being given manna in the wilderness they quoted Psalm 78:24, which says, "He gave them bread out of heaven to eat." Then Jesus said to them, "Very truly I tell you, it was not Moses who gave you the bread out of heaven, but it is my Father who gives you the true bread from heaven. For the bread of God is that which . . . gives life to the world." The followers answered, "Sir, give us this bread always." Jesus said to them, "I am the bread of life; Whoever comes to me will never be hungry and whoever believes in me will never be thirsty" (John 6:31–35 NRSV).

The Lord's Supper reminds us that God can spread a table for us in the wilderness. Jesus is our table in the wilderness. He is our bread of life. As he said, "This bread is my body, given for you. And this cup is my blood shed for you."

5

Love Is Best (RH)

The fifth-century-BC Greek poet Pindar began his first Olympic Ode with the words, "Water is best." He does not go on to discuss water in the poem, but speaks next of how gold is valued in human wealth, and then moves on to speak of the Olympic Games and to praise his patron who has won a prize at the games. We could speculate on precisely what Pindar wanted to convey by his opening words about water. Perhaps he wanted to put prizes and the wealth that it took to win them in proper perspective by noting first of all how such a common commodity as water far exceeds both honors and wealth in real value. Whether that was his intention or not, his statement is true. We do not live by gold and honors. We live by such a simple, common thing as water. Water is a basic ingredient of life. No form of life that we know can exist without water. "Water is best."

Paul makes a similar kind of statement at the end of 1 Corinthians 13. He has been discussing the subject of spiritual gifts. The church at Corinth had been fighting over spiritual gifts. Everyone, it seems, wanted a gift that called attention to themselves. They wanted especially to speak in tongues. Paul points out that there are a variety of gifts, not just one or two, and that everyone possesses some gift that will help build up the Christian community. Finally he says, "But strive for the greater gifts. *And I will show you a still more excellent way*" (1 Cor 12:31 NRSV, my emphasis). Then Paul devotes a long discussion to the praise of love. He concludes by singling out faith, hope, and love as the three most important qualities of a Christian and concludes, "but the greatest of these is love."

That strikes me as very similar to what Pindar does at the beginning of his first Olympic Ode. It was a big deal to win at the ancient Olympic Games, just as it still is. The particular winner Pindar is honoring in this poem was the king of Syracuse, who had won in the chariot races. There amid all the hoopla of winning at the Olympic Games he says to the winner, "Water is best." And in 1 Corinthians 13, amid all the hoopla over special gifts at Corinth, Paul says, "Love is best."

Just before his discussion of the wrangling over spiritual gifts that was going on in Corinth, Paul discusses the way the Corinthians were abusing the Lord's Supper. We have to remember that in the earliest days of the church Christians gathered in the evening and the Lord's Supper was celebrated at the close of a meal eaten together. Paul says that when they came together there were divisions and factions among them. It wasn't really to eat the Lord's Supper that they came together, he added, "For when the time comes to eat, each of you goes ahead with your own supper, and one goes hungry and another becomes drunk." He refers to this action as showing "contempt for the church of God" (1 Cor 11:21, 22 NRSV).

What was wrong with their participation in the Lord's Supper? There was no love among them. What Paul says about love in 1 Corinthians 13 is just as applicable to the way the Corinthians were divided and self-centered in their partaking of the Lord's Supper as it was to the way they were bickering over spiritual gifts. Paul doesn't think of the Lord's Supper as something that is just between me and the Lord. It is between me and all my brothers and sisters in the whole family of God—those who sit beside me, and behind me, and in front of me, and those I've never seen or ever will see in this life. The Lord's Supper is a communal meal, not a private snack. It says something about the relationship between me and my brothers and sisters in the Lord as well as *my* relationship to the Lord. It is something that we who are united in Christian love do together as a family. Water is best in the physical world, because there can be no physical life without it. In the church love trumps all things because there can be no church without it. Jesus said, "I give you a new commandment, that you love one another. Just as I have loved you, you also should love one another" (John 13:34 NRSV). As we remember Jesus at this table, let us also remember the "new commandment" that he gave to his disciples on his last night with them.

6

A Time to Forget (GK)

Memory is very important to life but there is something paradoxical about it. On the one hand, it is essential for our well-being that we can remember. But it is also essential for our well-being that we can forget.

Anyone who competes in athletic games knows the importance of forgetting. The golf professional Tom Watson had won the British Open several times but had not won for many years when, at age fifty-nine, he found himself leading after three rounds. He became the sentimental favorite, and everyone was pulling for him to win as he came to the last hole on the last day with a one-stroke lead. However, he made a couple of mistakes and ended in a tie with Stewart Cink. Watson was devastated and fell apart completely on the four-hole playoff, allowing Cink to win. Watson failed to forget what he had done, put it behind him, and look ahead to winning the playoff holes.

At the Lord's Table we often speak of remembering, and of course, we should, because Jesus said, "Do this in remembrance of me." On the other hand, when we come to the table it should also be a time of forgetting. We must not only remember God's saving grace in Christ, but we must also forget the past mistakes and failures that keep us from accepting his grace and moving on toward the future that God has for us.

Paul worked at doing this and said, "Beloved, I do not consider that I have made it my own; but this one thing I do: forgetting what lies behind and straining forward to what lies ahead, I press on toward the goal for the prize of the heavenly call of God in Christ Jesus" (Phil 3:13–14 NRSV).

At the Lord's Table we see with double vision. We look to the past and remember Jesus' sacrifice on our behalf, but we also look to the future and anticipate our destiny with him. As Paul put it in 1 Corinthians 11:26 (NRSV), speaking of our action in the Lord's Supper, "We proclaim the Lord's death until he comes." Remembering his death and what it means for us helps to wipe out the memory of our failures. It frees us to look to the future, to "press toward the goal" that Christ sets before us.

7

Giving Thanks (GK)

If you are asked unexpectedly to pray at your family's Thanksgiving gathering it might be well to avoid what one man did. Ben Witherington tells of a particular Thanksgiving dinner at his aunt's house in Statesville, North Carolina. "As we were all sitting down," he writes, "she asked my father to pray impromptu over the meal she had been preparing for many hours. Somewhat flustered and unprepared, he prayed, 'Dear Lord, please bless our sins and pardon this food in your Son's name. Amen.'" He would not soon live down that blessing, said Witherington.[1]

It is no surprise that a prayer on Thanksgiving Day, said with family gathered at a table covered with delicious food, would express heartfelt thanks. But what of other days, in other circumstances? Prayers have a way of getting to the heart of a matter. If you want to know how you feel about life, you might examine your prayers, especially prayers offered when you face a crisis of some kind.

Jesus was very much aware of the crisis he faced when he met with his apostles in the upper room. He knew the danger he was in. What was his prayer at that time? Three Gospels—Matthew, Mark, and Luke—along with Paul in 1 Corinthians 11, record what happened at that meal. There are variations in the wording, in the sequence of events, and in other aspects of their descriptions, but

1. Witherington, *Making a Meal*, 17.

one phrase is found to be the same in all accounts. It is simply this: "When he had given thanks . . ." Whatever the prayer went on to say, at the heart of Jesus' prayer was thanksgiving. Jesus must have been a thankful person at heart.

Through the centuries since then four terms, all found in the New Testament, have been used to name our observance. One is "the bread breaking," or "breaking of bread," based on Jesus' words and action in the upper room. Also, we call it "communion," which translates the Greek word, *koinona,* used by Paul in 1 Corinthians 10:16. We also call it "the Lord's Supper," based on the evening meal Jesus had with his disciples in the upper room. The fourth term, "Eucharist," is commonly used throughout the world. It comes from the phrase "when he had given thanks." This action by Jesus provided a model, not simply for a ritual but for a way of life, expressed in prayer.

Our ritual at the table should express a thanksgiving that carries over into all of life. The former secretary of the United Nations, Dag Hammarskjold, must have had that kind of outlook on life because shortly before his untimely death he said something that could very well be our prayer at this table, or on Thanksgiving Day, and at all times of life—especially times of crisis. He said simply, "For all that has been, thanks; for all that shall be, yes."[2]

2. Hammarskjold, *Markings,* 89.

8

Dressing Properly for Communion (GK)

As our pastor spoke on the Genesis account of when Adam and Eve were exposed and ashamed by their lack of clothing, I was struck by the verse that says, "And the Lord God made garments of skin for Adam and his wife and clothed them" (Gen 3:21 NIV). I often think of God as Father, or Shepherd, but had not thought of God as a fashion expert, a designer of clothing. I wonder, did Adam and Eve like to show off their Yahweh-designed clothing?

Then the question came to me, I wonder if God has designed clothing for us? And what does God expect me to wear when I come to the communion table? How can I dress properly for communion? Thinking about this gave me a fresh way of understanding some New Testament texts. I remembered that Paul sometimes used the metaphor of putting on clothes. He tells the Colossians that because they have "stripped off the old self with its practices and have clothed" themselves "with the new self" that is taking on "the image of its creator," they should put on "compassion, kindness, humility, meekness, and patience." Furthermore, they should be forgiving, just as they have been forgiven by the Lord. And above everything else, they should clothe themselves "with love" (Col 3:8–14 NRSV). In other places Paul summarizes all of this by simply saying, "Put on Christ" or "Clothe yourself with Christ."

Of course, Paul is talking about more than just Sunday-go-to-church clothes. These garments are meant to be worn every day. They will never go out of style, never wear out. In these clothes we will always look our best. There is something about putting on a new garment that fits perfectly, is made from the finest material, and is exactly the right color that makes us feel good. And we can be sure that God has designed the very best wardrobe for us.

Getting dressed like this is a process, not something we do once and for all. To "put on Christ" requires focusing on Christ in many ways and one of the most significant ways is in communion, regularly. At the table we continue the process of putting on Christ as we remember him, partake of the bread and the cup, and hear once again his words: "This bread is my body, given for you," and, "This cup is the new covenant in my blood, shed for the remission of sins."

9

Divine-Human Intersections (RH)

There is an interesting story about a minor character in the New Testament at the end of the first chapter of John's Gospel. Jesus is calling some of his disciples. He calls a man named Phillip, and Phillip immediately goes and finds his friend Nathanael. He says to Nathanael, we have found the one Moses and the prophets wrote about, Jesus from Nazareth. Nathanael replies skeptically, can any good thing come out of Nazareth? Phillip says, come and see. As the two men approach Jesus, Jesus looks at Nathanael and says, behold, an Israelite in whom there is no deceit, and Nathanael replies, how do you know me? Jesus says, before Phillip called you, I saw you under the fig tree. Nathanael replies, "Rabbi, You are the Son of God!" (John 1:49 NRSV). Nathanael is the first person to stand face-to-face with Jesus in John's Gospel and make that statement. In fact the only other person who does that in John's Gospel is Martha in chapter 11. Nathanael is a very minor personality in the New Testament. He is mentioned only twice in the entire New Testament—here at the end of John 1 and again at the beginning of John 21. In the latter passage he is named as one of the seven disciples present at the sea of Galilee after the resurrection when Jesus appears to some of the disciples. That is all there is to say about the backstory of Nathanael. The reason I am telling you this is to introduce the fascinating reply Jesus makes to Nathanael when Nathanael says, "You are the Son of God." Jesus replies, "Do you believe because I told you that I saw you under the fig tree? You will see greater things than these. . . . Very truly I tell you, you will see heaven opened and the angels of God ascending and descending upon the Son of Man" (John 1:50–51 NRSV).

I have to confess that Jesus' statement, "You will see heaven opened and the angels of God ascending and descending upon the Son of Man," has fascinated and puzzled me throughout my adult life as a minister and as a biblical scholar. First of all, is it a quotation? If it is, we do not know where it is found. It is usually referring to the vision that Jacob had in Genesis about dreaming of a ladder extending from earth to heaven with angels ascending and descending on it. Perhaps that is the reference. I do not know. But to what does it refer? There is no passage in the Gospels that speaks of angels ascending and descending on Jesus, and especially not of Nathanael seeing them. Matthew does say that angels came and ministered to Jesus at the end of his forty days of fasting and being tempted in the wilderness (Matt 4:11), but does not mention anyone being present and seeing the angels.

So what is Jesus saying here? I suspect that it is one of those statements of Jesus that he never intended anyone to understand literally—on a par with plucking out your right eye or cutting off your right hand to prevent certain actions.

N. T. Wright, in his little commentary on John's Gospel called *John for Everyone,* gives this saying of Jesus an intriguing application. John's Gospel, as you may know, is constructed around seven miracles Jesus worked, which John calls "signs." "The signs," Wright says, "are all occasions when Jesus did, you might say, what he'd just promised Nathanael that he would do. They are moments when, to people who watch with at least a little faith, the angels of God are going up and coming down at the place where Jesus is. They are moments when heaven is opened, when the transforming power of God's love bursts in to the present world. The whole point of the 'signs' is that they are moments when heaven and earth intersect with each other."[1]

---

1. Wright, *John,* 21.

I call this meditation "Divine-Human Intersections." These are not limited to the story told in the Gospels about Jesus' encounter with Nathanael. They are moments that happen all around us and to us when Jesus is present, and a different dimension of reality breaks into our lives—and the angels of God ascend and descend on the Son of Man.

The Lord's Supper can be one of those intersecting points when the divine breaks into our lives. Jesus took the loaf and the cup and said, "Do this in remembrance of me." And today, some two millennia later, we still do this in remembrance of him. And when we do it, it is an ordinary action with an extraordinary possibility. As one of the old communion hymns that the church used to sing puts it, "Here, O my Lord, I see Thee face to face, Here would I touch and handle things unseen."

IO

Enough! (GK)

In his book of meditations on the Psalms, Ben Patterson tells of a professor who was lecturing from Paul's letter, First Thessalonians, in which the apostle is teaching about the return of Christ. The professor was in Uganda and his students were young men preparing for ministry. These young men were living with horrendous reminders of what they had endured during the murderous reign of Idi Amin. Some were missing an eye or an arm. Several had bulging red scars from what had been deep machete wounds. In the eyes of all was the shadow of the horror they had seen. But there was also the light of the hope of Christ.

The professor read 1 Thessalonians 4:16: "The Lord himself will come down from heaven with a commanding shout, with the voice of the archangel, and the trumpet call of God." Immediately, a student's hand went up.

"Yes?" said the professor. "What is your question?"

The man who had raised his hand hesitated for a moment and then asked softly, "What will the Lord shout?"

The professor didn't know what to say. Who would? Yet the accumulated suffering of the students in that classroom seemed to demand some kind of answer. What will the Lord shout when he returns as Lord of Lords and King of Kings?

"I don't know," the professor admitted. Then he looked around the room, pausing to look at each student, and asked, "What do you think he will shout?"

A student's voice came from the back: "I think he will shout 'Enough!'" "That's a good answer," said the professor.[1] I agree. Enough violence, enough sickness and pandemics, enough tears, enough suffering, enough hatred. We all look forward to a time when all of this will be stopped and replaced with God's love.

Paul reminds us that the Lord's Supper looks forward to that time as he says, "For as often as you eat this bread and drink this cup, you proclaim the Lord's death until he comes" (1 Cor 11:26 NRSV). His words remind us that we look not only to the past with thanksgiving but to the future with hope. As we partake, we look to the future when he will return, and all will be well.

1. Patterson, *Prayer Book*, 184.

11

Why Bother (GK)

My friend Doug Priest was the pastor of a church not far from the one I served in northeast Oregon. We spent many happy hours hiking and fishing in the Eagle Cap wilderness area of the Wallowa Mountains. Then he and his wife and young children left the pastorate to become missionaries in Ethiopia.

I visited with him when they came home on furlough. He mentioned a problem they had in Ethiopia concerning the Lord's Supper. There were no grapes in their remote area. How do you have the Lord's Supper without grape juice? Or without wine from grapes? It was not feasible to ship it in. Instead, they used grape Kool-Aid. Some areas did not have Kool-Aid, so they used lemon juice. He also told me of missionaries he knew in Papua New Guinea where no flour was available to make bread, so they used sweet potatoes.

A more desperate situation was faced by J. Russell Morse when he was a missionary in Southern China. In 1951 he was arrested by the Communists and held in solitary confinement for fifteen months. He suffered many deprivations and was tortured both mentally and physically in ways that he never described even to his own family. For a long time, he expected each day to be his last. He said: "Back in my prison, I prepared to die, and I followed a procedure that I feel sure was followed by thousands in the early New Testament Church. . . . Daily, for months, I partook of those emblems, using steamed bread and water, which I had saved from my meals. And each day I prepared myself for that death which I thought might come at any hour."[1]

When I think of how so many Christians, in so many places, over hundreds of years have persisted in observing the Lord's Supper in whatever way they could, I have to ask, "Why bother?" Morse answered that question for himself, and for countless others when he said,

> I remember that [the early Christians] had been admonished to forsake not the assembling themselves. Also, in regard to the Lord's Supper, they had been told, "This do in remembrance of me," as they partook of the emblems of the Lord's broken body and shed blood. As they themselves faced death, they partook of them, remembering that he had been scourged by Roman soldiers; a crown of thorns had been pressed down upon his head; . . . He had been forced to carry his own cross upon which he soon was to be nailed to die there. And Jesus had said, "A servant is not greater than his Lord."

Why do we bother to come here each Sunday? Why do we bother to take the Lord's Supper? How would you answer?

1. Morse, *Dogs*, 304.

12

Grace for Help (RH)

"So that we may find grace to help in time of need" (Heb 4:16 NRSV), the Scripture reads. Or it could be translated, "So that we may find *grace for help at the moment that we need it*" (my translation). God has promised help when we need it, but it does not come until then. He did not divide the Red Sea three days before the Israelites arrived and hold the water back so that they would know in advance how he would deliver them. He had simply promised to be with them, to accompany them on their journey in a pillar of cloud by day and a pillar of fire by night. They had to trust that if God was traveling with them, there was no need to fear the Egyptians. He did not divide the Red Sea until Pharaoh's chariots were lined up on the horizon preparing to attack. When the Israelites were starving in the desert, God gave them manna to eat. But he did not give them a week's supply at the beginning of each week. They had to go out each day, gather only enough for that day, and trust God that there would be manna again tomorrow. Jesus taught us to pray, "Give us this day, our daily bread" (Matt 6:11 NRSV). I wonder if he was thinking of the manna when he said that.

The Israelites repeatedly doubted God's promise: at the Red Sea, in the desert when they were hungry or thirsty, but most seriously when they reached the Jordan River and the land God had promised to give them lay just on the other side. They learned of the fortified cities and the well-armed warriors on the other side of the Jordan, and they cried out, "Let's go back to Egypt." They had forgotten that *God* had promised to give them that land, and that he gives "grace for help at the moment that we need it."

We are not a lot like the Israelites; *we are exactly like them*! We forget what God has done for us in the past; we forget his mighty acts of salvation performed in Jesus of Nazareth and recorded in the New Testament. What did Jesus promise? "Lo, I am with you always even to the end of the age." Not so different from the promise of God to lead his people from Egypt into the land he promised to give them!

So because of our forgetful, prone-to-wander, human nature, God set up certain repetitious things as reminders of what he has done, and what he has promised to do. I think the necessity of gathering the manna daily must have been intended, partly at least, to remind the Israelites every day that it was God who was providing for them, and that he was faithful to his word, that they would find "grace for help at the moment" that they needed "it." And I am quite sure that this is the reason for this weekly gathering and partaking at the Lord's Table, for Jesus himself said, "This is my body that is for you. Do this in remembrance of me," and, "This cup is the new covenant in my blood. Do this, as often as you drink it, in remembrance of me. For as often as you eat this bread and drink the cup, you proclaim the Lord's death until he comes" (1 Cor 11:24–26 NRSV).

13

The Power of Story (RH)

The Jewish author Elie Wiesel, in his book *The Gates of the Forest,* tells a fascinating story about the power of story. He relates that there was a succession of rabbis in a village in Europe who were each faced by a crisis in the Jewish community they served and called on God for deliverance from the crisis. The first had a series of things that he performed that involved going into the forest, lighting a fire at a special place, and then asking God for deliverance for the community. When this had been done the crisis was averted. Each succeeding rabbi could remember less and less of what the previous rabbis had done and said. Finally the last rabbi, who could remember nothing of the previous rabbis' actions, said to God that all he could do was tell the story and that would have to be enough to save the community. Wiesel concludes that this was enough.[1]

Now I want to tell you a story from my own life when I was approximately three years old. We were living with my grandparents in a large farmhouse in western Illinois. It was during the great depression and World War II. We were in the large kitchen and my dad came in carrying a rooster by the legs—probably on its way to be slaughtered, I don't know. But the rooster began flapping its wings and making rooster noises. My mother teasingly said, "Run, Ronnie, run." And I replied, "I'm running as fast as I can," but I

---

1. Wiesel, *Gates of the Forest,* unnumbered front matter.

wasn't moving a muscle. I was petrified by the sound and sight of the rooster.

I can still see myself standing in my grandparents' kitchen and my dad holding the rooster. But I do not remember that event as an eyewitness even though it happened to me. As I said, I was perhaps three years old. *What I remember is the story* told over and over by my parents to different people when I was a kid, for a laugh. I don't remember the event; I remember the story, but the story keeps the event alive in my mind.

The Lord's Supper functions something like a story. We weren't there at the institution of the Lord's Supper, or the next day at the crucifixion. But we know the story; it is repeated for us each Lord's day at this table as we take the bread over which Jesus said, "This is my body; do this in remembrance of me," and the cup over which he said, "This is my blood of the covenant that is poured out for many for the forgiveness of sins."

There is an old gospel song that has the words, "Were you there when they crucified my Lord? . . . O, Sometimes it causes me to tremble. . . . Were you there when they crucified my Lord?" In a sense, we were there; and we are there as we remember, Sunday after Sunday, the story told by the loaf and the cup.

14

Imitate Me (GK)

When a man I had known for seventy years, a colleague in ministry, a companion on trips, a competitor on the golf course, and my best friend, died, I was asked to speak at his memorial service. As I thought about this I was, at the same time, thinking about what to say for a communion meditation on Sunday. These thoughts brought together several New Testament texts.

Second Timothy 4:7–8 (NAS) came to mind as I thought about my friend. Paul's words about himself seem also to characterize my friend: "I have fought the good fight, I have finished the course, I have kept the faith; in the future there is laid up for me the crown of righteousness, which the Lord, the righteous Judge will award to me on that day; and not only to me, but also to all who have loved his appearing." The idea of "finishing the course," reminded me of Jesus. At one point in his ministry, according to Luke 9:51 (NKJV), Jesus "set his face steadfastly to go to Jerusalem." He was determined to follow that course, and eventually, with a few stops along the way, he made it to Jerusalem. There, at the end of his journey he found a cross. As he hung upon that cross, having accomplished all that his Father sent him to do, Jesus said, "It is finished."

Why was Paul able to say what he did at the end of his life? I think much of the answer can be found in what he said earlier to the Corinthians. In 1 Corinthians 11:1 he urged them, "be imitators of me, just as I also imitate Christ." Paul tried to imitate Christ. He wanted to imitate his love, his forgiveness, his servanthood, even his sacrifice. Therefore, he said in Philippians 1:20–21 (NRSV), "It is my eager expectation and hope that I will not be put to shame in any way, but that by my speaking with all boldness, Christ will be exalted now as always in my body, whether by life or by death. For to me, living is Christ and dying is gain."

So Paul urged the Corinthians to imitate him as he imitated Christ. He went on in the same chapter to express his disappointment in how they were observing the Lord's Supper. They were not "discerning the body," that is the body of Christ. They were not living out what the Lord's Supper called for. They were not imitating the love of Christ, his forgiveness, his servanthood, and his sacrifice.

The call of the Lord's Supper has not changed. In it we can hear the voice of Christ himself saying, imitate me . . . imitate my love, imitate my forgiveness, imitate my servanthood, imitate my sacrifice. If we do that, we will be able to say with Paul at the end of our journey: "I have fought the good fight, I have finished the course, I have kept the faith."

15

Preparing for Communion (GK)

We can learn something from the actions of Jesus and his disciples that we see in Luke 22:7–13. Jesus knew that an extremely important event was coming, and preparation was needed. During his final week in Jerusalem, after he had cleansed the temple of money changers, Jesus knew that his life was in danger. Not wanting to go before he was ready, his usual routine was to spend the day among friendly crowds in the temple area and then move to safe lodging on the Mount of Olives. "In view of that," comments Fred Craddock, "one could easily read Jesus' instructions to Peter and John as intriguing prearrangements, as shadowy moves in a mystery novel."[1] "*A man carrying a jar of water will meet you; follow him*" (Luke 22:10 NRSV, emphasis added), Jesus said. It was unusual for a man to carry water; that was a woman's work, and so the man would be easily spotted. Apparently, Jesus knew of a house where they could safely meet and had arranged to use it. He had prepared for this moment.

He also gave instructions to make further preparation. The Passover meal was coming and this required purchasing bread, wine, herbs, and a lamb that had been approved by a priest as unblemished and properly slain. The lamb was then roasted. There was a lot of preparation, which signified the importance of the

1. Craddock, *Luke*, 254.

event. When something is important, we prepare carefully. As a result of their meeting in that upper room we have this action of communion and remembrance.

Wouldn't it be good for us to think more about our preparation? I do not mean the mechanics of supplying and filling trays. I mean our preparation to participate. Primarily, this requires a certain mindset, a matter of focusing on our purpose for coming together. As we get ready at home, we could say to ourselves, I am preparing to meet with my Lord at the table. As we meet and greet one another we could think about the theme of oneness found in the Lord's Supper. As we sing and pray in worship, we could see it leading us to the table.

Every Sunday our pastor presents a well-prepared sermon. We too should come well prepared to meet with our Lord.

16

Grace and Snow (RH)

We awoke several weeks ago to a blanket of snow on the ground and it continued to fall through a big part of the day. I apologize for making you think of snow at a time of year when you are more likely thinking of daffodils. But I want us to think about snow briefly, because grace is a lot like snow.

Grace, like snow, usually comes silently. You do not normally associate thunder and lightning with a snowfall. Snow just floats gently and silently to the ground. Grace is like that. You often do not know when you are experiencing it. It does not usually slap you in the face and you shout out, "Wow! I was just hit by a load of grace!" No, it just gently floats down into our lives. It's like Elijah's encounter with God on Mount Horeb. Remember that after all the fireworks of Elijah's contest with the prophets of Baal, he was feeling like he was on top of the world—God had just demonstrated his power before the people by sending down fire when Elijah had prayed for it. Then Queen Jezebel decided to have him killed because he had destroyed her prophets of Baal. Elijah had to go into hiding in the mountains and while there, feeling very sorry for himself, he had an encounter with God. The biblical author describes it this way: "Now there was a great wind, so strong that it was splitting mountains and breaking rocks in pieces before the Lord, but the Lord was not in the wind; and after the wind an earthquake, but the Lord was not in the earthquake; and after the earthquake a fire, but the Lord was not in the fire; and after the fire, *a sound of sheer silence*" (1 Kings 19:11–12 NRSV, my emphasis). Then the Lord spoke to Elijah and reassured him. As someone once said, God can shout, but he prefers to whisper. Grace usually comes into our lives silently, like snow. As Philip Brooks wrote in his hymn "O Little Town of Bethlehem":

> How silently, how silently, The wondrous gift is given!
> So God imparts to human hearts The blessings of His heaven.

Grace is also like snow because it covers all things and makes them beautiful. It's very hard to beat the beauty of a fresh snowfall, when everything looks white and clean and pure. Grace is like that. It covers our sins, no matter how ugly they may have been. The ancient Hebrew prophet Isaiah saw this connection. "Though your sins are like scarlet," he said, "they shall be like snow" (Isa 1:18 NRSV).

There is one other similarity between grace and snow. Snow can be dangerous. Why does the highway patrol recommend staying off the roads when there is snow? You know the answer to that. It's dangerous to drive in snow. You have to drive differently than you do when the roads are clear and dry, and if you don't there's a good chance that you will wind up in a ditch or in an accident. Snow can be dangerous. But is grace dangerous? Potentially, yes. Grace always brings responsibility with it. It's not a "get-out-of-jail-free" card like in the old Monopoly game. It always comes with the expectation that there will be change. When Isaiah spoke in the name of the Lord to the Israelites and told them that their sins could be made "like snow," he didn't add, "And you may go on doing what you have been doing in your rebellion against the Lord." No, his next words were, "*If* you are willing and obedient, you shall eat the good of the land; but *if* you refuse and rebel, you shall be devoured by the sword; for the mouth of the Lord has spoken" (Isa 1:19–20 NRSV, my emphasis). Or, as Paul put it in Romans: "Do you not realize that God's kindness is meant to lead you to repentance?" (Rom 2:4 NRSV). Grace is like snow. It comes unobtrusively and it can change the whole complexion of our lives, but we have to receive it graciously, responsibly, and thankfully.

Each Sunday we gather at this table to celebrate and give thanks for this marvelous gift of God's grace, given to us through the life, death, and resurrection of his Son. We partake of the bread of which Jesus said, "This is my body," and we drink from the cup over which Jesus said, "This is my blood of the covenant, which is poured out for many for the forgiveness of sins" (Matt 26:26, 28 NRSV).

17

When Heaven Came Down (RH)

The prophet Isaiah prayed a fervent, but somewhat unusual, prayer when he intoned, "O that you would tear open the heavens and come down, so that the mountains would quake at your presence" (Isa 64:1 NRSV).

The apostle John tells us that God has done precisely that. He has come down. "In the beginning was the Word," John says, "and the Word was with God, and the Word was God. . . . And the Word became flesh and lived among us, and we have seen his glory" (John 1:1, 14 NRSV). But after those opening verses of John's Gospel, we don't see much glory as we read further. John relates seven miracles that Jesus worked. After the first of these he comments, "Jesus did this, . . . and revealed his glory; and his disciples believed in him" (John 2:11 NRSV).

But Jesus always refused to do anything special when people would press him to show them a sign. Most of the first half of John's Gospel is taken up with Jesus teaching disciples and arguing with the religious establishment in Jerusalem. It's in the last half of his Gospel that John presents Jesus' glory. But John has a special understanding of glory. Words like "glory" and "glorify" are sprinkled about freely in John's text, starting with chapter 12. For John the glorification of Jesus is his death and resurrection. In the prayer

Jesus prayed in John 17, shortly before he would be arrested, condemned and crucified, he said, "Father, the hour has come; glorify your Son so that the Son may glorify you" (John 17:1 NRSV). The "hour" here refers to the crucifixion of Jesus.

In the fourth century AD, Athanasius, bishop of Alexandria in Egypt, closed his address to those who had been baptized on Easter Sunday with these words: "Let us expect to see Christ rising, bearing trophies from the tomb, bearing the victory over death and the devil. Therefore, let us, *beaming with joy*, approach the resurrected Christ. For all glory, honor, and praise is appropriate for him, with the Father and the Holy Spirit, for ever and ever."[1] Or, as the German theologian Jürgen Moltmann paraphrased those last words, "Christ, risen from the dead, makes the whole of human life a festival without end."[2]

God has opened heaven and come down, and all of human life has become a festival. We celebrate that every Sunday as we gather in the name of Jesus to praise him, and especially as we partake of the bread and cup of this table. For on the night of his betrayal Jesus took bread, blessed it, broke it, and gave it to his disciples saying, "Take, eat, this is my body. Then he took a cup, and after giving thanks he gave it to them, saying, Drink from it, all of you; for this is my blood of the covenant, which is poured out for many for the forgiveness of sins. I tell you, I will never again drink of this fruit of the vine until that day when I drink it new with you in my Father's kingdom" (Matt 26:27–29 NRSV).

1. Migne, ed., *Patrologiae Graecae* 28, 1061b, my translation.
2. Moltmann, *Living God,* 192.

18

Mission and the Lord's Supper (GK)

The church's mission and the Lord's Supper are vitally linked. Jesus spelled out our mission when he said, "Go into all the world and proclaim the good news to the whole creation" (Mark 16:15 NRSV). The good news is centered in God's gift of Jesus Christ—his death and resurrection. Paul put it this way: "If, while we were enemies, we were reconciled to God through the death of his Son, much more surely, having been reconciled, will we be saved by his life" (Rom 5:10 NRSV). The proclamation of this good news is our mission. Paul makes the connection between this mission and the Lord's Supper clear when he says in 1 Corinthians 11:26 (NRSV), "For as often as you eat this bread and drink this cup, you proclaim the Lord's death until he comes."

It has been said that a picture is worth a thousand words. If true, the visible sermon we proclaim at the Lord's Table is far more powerful than the word spoken from the pulpit. My parents may have sensed this. At Milwaukie, when I was a boy, we had one of the best preachers around. He later became nationally known among our churches. Occasionally, we would leave church early to visit my grandparents in Forest Grove. But we never left before communion. Apparently, my parents felt we could miss the sermon but not communion. They didn't articulate that to us kids, but as I look back, I realize that their example impressed upon me how vitally important it is that the whole church gather every Lord's Day to "proclaim the Lord's death."

Beyond engaging in the very essence of mission—proclaiming the redemptive sacrifice of Christ—there is another affect on our mission that comes from faithful observance of the Lord's Supper. It provides nourishment for the work of mission. Tom Wright, theologian, professor, pastor, and prolific writer, wrote of what the Eucharist meant to him: "When I was engaged in regular pastoral ministry I found that the only way I could cope with the daily demands was the daily Eucharist. There I could lay all my puzzles and problems symbolically before God and find them not removed but reshaped in the pattern of Jesus."[1]

Set as it is in the heart of worship, and in conjunction with the spoken word, our communion with Christ provides a silent sermon along with the renewal and resources that we need for mission.

---

1. Wright, *Making a Meal*, 76.

19

The Table of Beginning Again (GK)

I will confess my sins—as a golfer. I must confess that I am often guilty, in a golfing sense, of sinfulness. The biblical word for sin means "missing the mark." When you swing a forty-four-inch club at great speed and try to hit a very small object, it is not unusual to miss the mark. Even the best golfers often miss. Follow any top professional around the course and you will see him fail to hit the ball perfectly many times. In golf, as in life, "all sin and fall short."

One of the things I like about golf is that you get to start over again regularly. So, you mess up on the first hole. Okay, just go to the next tee and start again. Regularly you can begin again. You can leave the missed hits behind and start over. In a full round of golf, you have seventeen second chances.

In life, also, we need opportunities to begin again. Jesus gave people such opportunities. Some, like Zacchaeus, eagerly accepted the chance to begin life anew (Luke 19:1–10). We don't know how she responded but Jesus certainly gave the woman caught in adultery a chance to start over when he did not condemn her but said, "go your way and from now on do not sin again" (John 8:11 NRSV). Sadly, some turned him down, but Jesus was always ready to help anyone begin again.

One of the reasons I like having the Lord's Supper every Sunday is that it gives me the opportunity on a regular basis to leave behind the missed hits and begin again. Paul spoke of "forgetting what lies behind and straining forward to what lies ahead" (Phil 3:13 NRSV). It is good in golf that the opportunity comes frequently. I wouldn't want to play a par forty hole instead of a par four. There would be a lot of missed hits before I could regroup and start again. Likewise, it is good that we can come frequently to the Lord's Table, acknowledge our missed hits, confess our sins, find forgiveness, and start the new week with a clean slate.

We call this the Table of Remembrance, but it could also be called the Table of Beginning Again. I know there are other means available to us to find forgiveness and renewal, but I like the idea that Jesus meets us here every week and says, This is my body given for you; this is my blood of the covenant shed for the forgiveness of sins. God must have known that we would need a regular opportunity to begin again, and this is it.

20

Our Story (GK)

On the Fourth of July we remember the birth of our nation. Wanting to know more about the birth and growth of our nation, I have read several biographies of presidents and other important figures who were present during the early years of our nation. These stories have helped me understand more fully who we are as Americans.

Stories play a powerful role in our lives. They entertain and teach us. They preserve culture and pass on cultural knowledge from one generation to another. Perhaps the greatest role that stories play in our lives is that they form and reveal who we are. Stories form and express our beliefs and values. Stories create and shape our worldview and can also change it.

While living in Oklahoma, I heard that many years ago a Native American child was taken to his grandmother's home and left with her for several days. She spent that time telling him stories, the stories of his people. He went there not thinking about who he was; he left knowing that he was a Kiowa.

Stories come out of our past, out of what has already happened, which is why history is so important. Psalm 105, and several others, demonstrate how important Israel's history was to it. Psalm 105 opens with a series of imperatives: "Give thanks to the Lord, call on his name . . . make known his deeds . . . sing praises to him . . . tell of all his wondrous works . . . glory in his holy name . . .

seek the Lord . . . remember the wonderful works he has done" (Ps 105:1–5 NRSV).

"Remember!" it says, and then proceeds to tell Israel's story, beginning with the covenant God made with Abraham and continuing with the time in Egypt and the miraculous exodus. Why was it important, centuries later, for Jewish families to tell Israel's story over and over again? Why was it important for Israel to periodically reenact that story during elaborate feasts and festivals? Because that story made and told them who they were. It gave them their way of life, their ethics, their faith, and set the direction for their journey in the world.

The story of God's saving acts throughout history, culminating in the coming of Jesus, the master storyteller, has become our story. First Peter 2:9–10 (NRSV) uses ancient texts from Israel's story to summarize how that story identifies us: "You are a chosen race, a royal priesthood, a holy nation, God's own people, in order that you may proclaim the mighty acts of him who called you out of darkness into his marvelous light. Once you were not a people, but now you are God's people; once you had not received mercy but now have received mercy."

The Lord's Supper is one of the stories that identify us as those who have been chosen, have received mercy, and now are the people of God. We acknowledge that when in our worship we say together the confession of faith: *I believe that Jesus is the Christ, the Son of the living God, and my Lord and Savior.*

21

The Lamb of God (RH)

I want to think very briefly about three passages of Scripture: the first is in the Gospel of John, the second is in the book of the prophet Isaiah, and the third is in the Apocalypse or Revelation of John the seer. These three passages together give us a thumbnail sketch of what we celebrate here at this table.

In John 1:29 (NRSV), John the Baptist sees Jesus coming toward him, and says to those who are with him, "Here is the Lamb of God who takes away the sin of the world!" What a strange way to introduce someone! If I were to introduce you, I would give your name, perhaps where you are from, and perhaps what you do. But John doesn't say, "Here is Jesus, a prophet (or a teacher) from Nazareth." He says, "Here is the Lamb of God who takes away the sin of the world." John's introduction of Jesus bypasses all the mundane information that we associate with a person and is packed with imagery from the Old Testament that identifies Jesus as the central figure in God's plan to redeem the world.

It was not common in the ancient world to refer to someone as a lamb, nor was it particularly flattering to do so. Sheep in general were known for their helplessness, and lambs were the most helpless of the sheep. The lamb was a symbol of weakness. In Luke 10:3 (NRSV) Jesus says to his disciples, "I am sending you out like lambs into the midst of wolves." There is no better imagery for total helplessness and weakness than that of a lamb surrounded by a pack of wolves. The lamb's chances of survival in that situation are zero.

There is a significant lamb passage in the Old Testament that quite probably influenced John's statement about Jesus being "the lamb of God who takes away the sin of the world." This is Isaiah 53:7, but the description begins in Isaiah 53:5 with the words, "But he was wounded for our transgressions, crushed for our iniquities; upon him was the punishment that made us whole, and by his bruises we are healed. All we like sheep have gone astray; we have all turned to our own way, and the Lord has laid on him the iniquity of us all." And then in verse 7 Isaiah says, "He was oppressed, and he was afflicted, yet he did not open his mouth; like a lamb that is led to the slaughter, . . . he did not open his mouth." The passage goes on to say, "yet he bore the sin of many, and made intercession for the transgressors" (Isa 53:5–7 NRSV). "Here is the lamb of God who takes away the sin of the world."

Now we go to Revelation chapter 5. In Revelation 4 the Lord God is worshipped by all the heavenly beings in the song, "You are worthy, our Lord and God, to receive glory and honor and power, for you created all things, and by your will they existed and were created" (Rev 4:11 NRSV).

Then in Revelation 5 God holds a sealed scroll, and an angel cries out, "Who is worthy to open the scroll and break its seals?" No one in all heaven was found worthy to take the book and open the seals. Then, John, who is the recipient of the vision, sees "between the throne and the four living creatures and among the elders a Lamb standing as if it had been slaughtered. . . . He went and took the scroll from the right hand of the one who was seated on the throne." When the lamb had "taken the scroll," John says, "the four living creatures and the twenty-four elders fell before the Lamb. . . . They sing a new song: 'You are worthy to take the scroll and to open its seals, for you were slaughtered and by your blood you ransomed for God saints from every tribe and language and people and nation; you have made them to be a kingdom and priests serving our God.'" Then John hears the voice of myriads of angels "singing with full voice, 'Worthy is the lamb that was slaughtered to receive power and wealth and wisdom and might and honor and glory and blessing!'" Finally, John hears another thunderous song. He hears "every creature in heaven and on earth and under the earth and in the sea . . . singing, 'To the one seated on the throne *and to the Lamb* be blessing and honor and glory and might forever and ever! And the four living creatures said, 'Amen'. And the elders fell down and worshiped" (Rev 5:2, 6, 7, 8, 9, 10, 12, 13–14 NRSV, my emphasis).

In this final picture John's lamb of God "who takes away the sin of the world" has been exalted to the throne room of God and is worshipped along with God by all creatures in heaven and on earth. This is the One we celebrate at this table! "Here is the lamb of God who takes away the sin of the world."

22

Strength in Unity (GK)

I have heard it said that the church is like a chain, having many individuals linked together. I don't like this image of the church because of its implications. A chain is only as strong as its weakest link. What happens in the church when the weakest link breaks? Are the rest able to continue their work? I don't like this image because it negates the strength of the other links. A better image has been suggested—that of a cable, which consists of many wires. If one wire becomes frayed or weakened in some way, and even if it should snap, the other wires with their combined strength would still carry on their work.

Each strand is weak, just as individual members of the body have their weaknesses. But, as Ecclesiastes says, "Two are better than one . . . and a threefold cord is not quickly broken" (Eccl 4:9, 12 NRSV). The cable, with many strands making it stronger than any one strand, is a more scriptural image of the church. It speaks of the unity of the church, of each member supporting the others, and of the church banding together to accomplish God's will.

Paul expresses this principle in Galatians 6:1–2 (NRSV), "My friends, if anyone is detected in a transgression, you who have received the Spirit should restore such a one in a spirit of gentleness. Take care that you yourselves are not tempted. Bear one another's burdens, and in this way, you will fulfill the law of Christ."

The Lord's Supper symbolizes the nature of the church as it pictures unity—the oneness in which we support each other. Paul put it this way in 1 Corinthians 10:16–17 (NAS), "Is not the cup of blessing which we bless a sharing in the blood of Christ? Is not the bread which we break a sharing in the body of Christ? Since there is one bread, we who are many are one body; for we all partake of the one bread."

The very way we observe the feast speaks of this unity. It used to be the practice of many churches to express unity by using only one cup. Those days are long gone, and a variety of practices have developed. In my church each of us has his or her own wafer and cup of juice. When the leader recites the words of institution, "This is my body given for you," we partake of the bread simultaneously. In like manner, we partake together following the words of institution for the cup. The oneness of action symbolizes the unity of God's people. The way each church does it may vary but it is important to symbolize the one body of Christ as we partake of his body and blood.

23

Our Toast (GK)

Coming out of the Great Depression and the Prohibition era as devout Christians, my family was not a drinking family. I don't remember ever seeing my parents drink an alcoholic beverage. Frances and I continued the no-drinking policy as we raised our children. I don't regret this policy and would do it again, for several reasons which I will not go into here. However, I realize now that by not having a glass of wine with our meal we missed out on a rich and universal custom. Henri Nouwen describes it this way:

> After a meal the wine is poured. No one drinks until all are served. Then all lift their cups, look each other in the eye, and offer a toast. It is a universal (and ancient) custom. In Latin the toast is "prosit," ("be well"); in German, "zum wohl," ("to your well-being"); in English, "cheers"; in Polish, "sto lat" ("a hundred years"); in Ukrainian, "na zdornis," ("to your health"); and in Hebrew, "L Chaim," ("to life!").[1]

The Hebrew toast is an old one, but I don't know how old. I have wondered if it was the custom in Jesus' day to lift the cup and say, "To life!" We do know that in the Passover meal, which Jesus and the disciples ate in the upper room, there were traditionally four cups that were used. The third came, as Luke says, "after

---

1. Nouwen, *Can You Drink?*, 57.

supper," and was called in Jewish tradition, "the cup of blessing." When Jesus held it before them Luke says that he added this unique statement: "This cup that is poured out for you is the new covenant in my blood" (Luke 22:20 NRSV). When Paul referred to it in 1 Corinthians 10:16 he used the Jewish phrase "the cup of blessing" (NRSV). Paul must have called it the cup of blessing not only because it was traditional, but because it meant for him that we are taking into ourselves the very life of Jesus.

It would be quite appropriate then for all of us to take the cup, hold it up, look into each other's eyes and say, "TO LIFE!"

To life without guilt!

To life without fear!

To life without end!

As Jesus himself said, "I came that they may have life, and have it abundantly" (John 10:10 NRSV). As we lift the cup of blessing, we can say, "To Life!"—Yes, to Life with a capital "L."

24

"What we have seen and touched with our hands" (RH)

In the opening words of the first letter of John the author makes a rather unusual statement. "We declare to you," he says, "what was from the beginning, what we have heard, what we have seen with our eyes, what we have looked at and touched with our hands, concerning the word of life" (1 John 1:1 NRSV). Notice how many of our senses he appeals to in that statement: hearing, seeing, and touching.

We tend to limit our understanding of Christian faith to intellectual ideas conveyed to our mind by reading or listening to sermons or lectures. Those are important and I would not downplay them. But we rarely consider that the Christian faith is also communicated through and to our other senses as well. For Jesus' disciple Thomas, his faith in the resurrected Christ came through the sense of touch. You remember his doubt when some of the disciples said they had seen Jesus alive after his crucifixion. Thomas needed to see and touch the wounds in Christ's body. Jesus didn't castigate Thomas when he appeared to the disciples again. He said instead, "Put your finger here and see my hands. Reach out your hand and put it in my side." And Thomas believed! "My Lord and my God," (John 20:27, 28 NRSV) he said. Do you suppose Thomas ever had doubts about Jesus being alive again?

Often our nonintellectual senses communicate things to us far more vividly than reading or hearing about something. One time when we were living in Germany and I was on one of my early morning runs, I was running on a path that went along the edge of a farm field. The farmer had cut the hay in that field, perhaps the day before, and it was lying in the field drying. The smell of that particular hay freshly cut took me back immediately to my childhood on the farm in western Illinois. It was so vivid that it was nearly shocking. I can remember telling my wife about the experience when I got back to the apartment. A smell, a sound, a taste, any of these can bring a whole flood of memories to our minds. Remember the psalmist said, "Taste and see that the Lord is good" (Ps 34:8 NRSV).

Jesus quite intentionally chose to communicate the deepest, most mysterious meaning of his life and death through the senses of touch and taste. In Matthew's account of the institution of the Lord's Supper, Jesus takes a loaf of bread, blesses it, breaks it, gives it to the disciples, and says, "Take, eat [touch, taste] this is my body." Then, Matthew says, "He took a cup, and after giving thanks he gave it to them, saying, Drink from it, all of you; for this is my blood of the covenant, which is poured out for many for the forgiveness of sins" (Matt 26:27, 28 NRSV). Touch and taste and remember the deepest mystery of the Christian faith—Jesus' redemptive death for sinful humanity.

25

The Medicine of Immortality (GK)

John 6:54 (NRSV) records a remarkable statement by Jesus: "Those who eat my flesh and drink my blood have eternal life, and I will raise them up on the last day." Ignatius of Antioch, an early church leader, may have known the apostle John at Ephesus and would have been acquainted with his teaching. Shortly after the turn of the first century Ignatius was the bishop of the church at Antioch of Syria. He was arrested by the Roman authorities and sent to Rome, where he died in the Colosseum as a Christian martyr during the reign of Emperor Trajan. As Ignatius traveled toward Rome he wrote several letters, and one was sent to Ephesus. He may have had the words of Jesus as reported by John in mind when he referred to the Lord's Supper in his letter to the Ephesians as "the medicine of immortality, the antidote we take in order not to die but to live forever in Jesus Christ."[1]

Some time ago, I remembered his words in the middle of the night. I had just seen my primary care doctor for a physical exam. I have been blessed with good health and had not seen my doctor for a long time. Strangely, after getting a good report, within two weeks I was struck down by a vicious bug, then a sprained shoulder muscle, and then an attack of asthmatic bronchitis. I don't like

1. Ignatius, Ephesians 20.2, in *Apostolic Fathers*, 199.

being sick. I am not used to it. Reluctantly, I went back to my doctor and the pharmacist.

Sin is like a sickness in several ways. Sin, like sickness, affects all of us. Is there anyone who has not been sick? It's the same with sin. As Paul said, "All have sinned and fall short of the glory of God" (Rom 3:23 NRSV). Sin is also like a sickness because it leaves us feeling terrible. We hurt in a lot of ways. And sin is like a sickness because it makes us do what we don't want to do and keeps us from doing what we want to do. Paul said exactly that in Romans 7 and then raised the plaintive question: "Wretched man that I am! Who will rescue me from this body of death?" (Rom 7:24 NRSV). This points to another similarity. Sin, like sickness, leads to death. If one sickness doesn't get us another will. And of course, the Scriptures are clear on the ultimate affect of sin. As Paul said in Romans 5:12 (NRSV), "Death spread to all because all have sinned."

When Paul asked in Romans 7:24 (NRSV), "Who will rescue me from this body of death?" he answered his question immediately with the exclamation, "Thanks be to God through Jesus Christ our Lord."

Sin, like sickness, requires both a physician and a pharmacist. In Jesus Christ we have both. As we come to him at the table, he is our good physician who provides for us "the medicine of immortality." He himself is that medicine. He meets us at the table. We hear again his words: "This bread is my body, given for you; this cup is the new covenant in my blood, shed for you." And we also remember his words, "Whoever eats my flesh and drinks my blood has eternal life."

26

The Gospel Every Week (GK)

I once had a student at Northwest Christian College (now Bushnell University) who asked me the same question several times. He was an older student, from the Midwest, had a good sense of humor, and with his Reformed Church background enjoyed playing a little game with me. The question always came if we happened to see each other as we left a chapel service. "Was that gospel or law?" he would ask, referring to the sermon we had just heard. He knew the answer and he knew that I knew the answer, but he liked to play that little game.

If someone asked you after today's service, "was that sermon gospel or law?" what would you say? It might help if I define the terms. By "law" I do not mean legalistic rules and regulations. In this case, it means guidance and helpful instructions for living. It is the kind of guidance found in the Sermon on the Mount or in some of the epistles. It is the biblical revelation of God's will for our lives. The sermon might provide helpful guidance on loving one another, or on living a holy life, or how to pray, but it would not be a gospel sermon. The gospel is not good advice or good ideas or good instruction. The gospel is good news.

What is the "good news"? In its simplest and most essential sense it is Christ. To preach Christ is to preach the gospel. The gospel, Paul declares, is what saves us, and gives a concise summary of it in 1 Corinthians 15:1–4 (NKJV):

Moreover, I declare to you the gospel which I preached to you, which also you received and in which you stand, by which also you are saved, if you hold fast that word which I preached to you—unless you believed in vain. For I delivered to you first of all that which also I received: that Christ died for our sins according to the Scriptures, and that he was buried, and that he rose again the third day according to the Scriptures, and that he was seen by Cephas, then by the twelve."

The content of the gospel is: Christ; Christ predicted in the Scriptures; Christ crucified for our sins and buried; Christ resurrected and seen to be alive.

The great Reformer and theologian John Calvin believed that we need the gospel preached to us every week, and the Lord's Supper to ratify the promise, because we are partly unbelievers until we die. We are like the distraught father who said to Jesus, "Lord, I believe, help my unbelief" (Mark 9:24 NRSV). We are all partly unbelievers and we need to hear the gospel every week—the good news of what God has done for us in Christ, his sacrifice for our forgiveness and salvation.

The sermon may be "law," in the best sense of that word, but not "gospel." Still, we hear the gospel weekly in the service of communion. The meditation, the words of institution, the confession of faith, and the action of partaking all proclaim the good news of Christ.

27

Waiting on the Lord (RH)

Jesus' last words to his disciples in the Gospel of Luke are, "Behold, I am sending the promise of my Father upon you; but stay in the city until you are clothed with power from the Highest" (Luke 24:49, my translation).

In other words, Wait. Can you imagine how difficult that must have been? The disciples had just witnessed and participated in the most extraordinary events in their lives, or in the lives of anyone, in fact. They had finally caught the vision of who Jesus of Nazareth really was. What do they want to do? They want to get back to Galilee and tell those old fishermen buddies about it. Go somewhere! Do something! Don't just sit idle in Jerusalem. But Jesus says, "Wait." Wait for God's power. How long did they have to wait? We do not know precisely, but the crucifixion was at Passover time and the divine power came at Pentecost, which was fifty days after Passover. That was nearly two months! I can imagine them starting to ask one another after a day or two, "Have you noticed any extraordinary power yet?" "No, have you?" But when God's time was right, there was no question that the power had come.

Waiting is hard. It is usually harder than acting. I used to have a colleague who would say in jest when we were sitting around talking, "Come on, let's go do something, even if it's wrong." And it usually is when we take the bit in our mouths and attempt to run ahead of God.

Have you ever noticed how often in the Bible people are told to wait for the Lord? In Exodus 24:12 (NRSV) the Lord says to Moses, "Come up to me on the mountain and wait there. . ." Moses did, and it was six days before the Lord appeared to him. Psalm 27:14 (NRSV) exhorts us, "Wait for the Lord; be strong, and let your heart take courage; wait for the Lord!" In Psalm 37:7 (NRSV) we are told to "Be still before the Lord, and wait patiently for him." That command is frequent in the Psalms and in Isaiah. Isaiah 40:31 (NRSV), for example, says, "But those who wait for the Lord shall renew their strength, they shall mount up with wings like eagles, they shall run and not be weary, they shall walk and not faint." Wait for the Lord. It's a hard discipline to learn.

The Lord's Supper is about waiting for the Lord. It is certainly about remembering Jesus, but it is also a subtle reminder that we are waiting for him to return. All the descriptions of the Lord's Supper in the New Testament contain references to a future reuniting with Jesus when we will eat and drink with him. Paul makes the reminder most explicit when he says, "For as often as you eat this bread and drink the cup you proclaim the Lord's death *until he comes*" (1 Cor 11:26 NRSV, my emphasis).

28

The Lord of Life (GK)

Long before Christianity came to northern Europe and the British Isles, October 31 and November 1 were special days for the Celtic people. These days marked the death of summer and beginning of winter. The Celts recognized this with a special feast named for the Celtic Lord of Death, Samhain (Sow-een). His name meant "summer's end." It was not, however, a happy occasion. Since winter is the season of cold, darkness, and death, the Celts soon made the connection with human death. The Eve of Samhain, October 31, was a time of Celtic pagan sacrifice, and a time when Lord Samhain allowed the souls of the dead to return to their earthly homes. Ghosts, witches, goblins, and elves came and frightened people. In Ireland people held a parade in which they followed a leader in a white robe with a mask from the head of an animal. They went door to door asking for food. The Scots walked through fields and villages carrying torches and lit bonfires to ward off witches and other evil spirits. From sunset on October 31, when their day began, the Lord of Death reigned supreme.

Sometime after the Celts began honoring the Lord of Death a very different feast began in the Mediterranean world. It too focused on death, but in a very different way. At first, it was a day to commemorate martyrs who had been killed because they refused to denounce Christ and worship the emperor. Later it expanded to remember and honor those special people named saints by the church. Eventually, the church recognized what Paul knew from the beginning—that all who profess faith in Christ are saints. They are—we are—the holy people of God. Several dates were used at first but eventually the church settled on November 1 for the Feast of All Saints' Day.

When the church came to England and spread throughout Northern Europe, the Anglo-Saxon word "Hallows" was the name used for the feast. They called it, "All Hallows' Day," and the evening before was called "Halloween." We still use this word in the Lord's Prayer: "Hallowed be your name . . ." (Matt 6:9 NRSV).

The two traditions, the feasts of Samhain and All Saints' Day, clashed and are still in conflict today. For the Christian the question must be faced: who do I honor today, the Lord of Death or the Lord of Life? Is my focus on the unholy, the dark and scary things of death, on ghosts and goblins, werewolves, and zombies, or on the Holy One who not only died for us but was raised to new life? Our confession of faith answers that question as we meet the Lord of Life at his table. Here we honor and remember the Lord of Life. And we do it with all the saints. My long life and service in many churches has allowed me to know a lot of saints. I wish I could name all of them now, because I feel, as Hebrews 12:1 (NRSV) says, "surrounded" by "so great a cloud of witnesses," those who have passed on and those still living, who have chosen on this day to honor the Lord of Life. We can join them at the table in remembering and honoring the Lord of Life by saying together one of the great creeds of the church or even the simple confession of belief in Jesus as the Christ and our savior.

29

The Good Shepherd (RH)

I grew up on a farm in western Illinois. We had cows, pigs, horses, chickens, cats, and dogs, but no sheep. Few people in that area of the country raised sheep. My cousin had a sheep for his 4-H project, and that was as close as I came to any experience with sheep when I was a child. Whenever I saw sheep they were always enclosed by fences, and there was never a shepherd with them. The farmer simply put them in a fenced field and left them.

I was intrigued, therefore, when I began travelling and working in Eastern Europe in the early 1980s to see shepherds. I recall driving through the former Yugoslavia, and seeing flocks of sheep in open fields without fences and a shepherd standing near them leaning on a long staff. When we lived in Tübingen, Germany each summer a local shepherd pastured his sheep on the Òsterberg, a huge hill behind my office building that I could see from my window. He would stay on that hillside with his sheep all day long.

After observing shepherds in Europe, I can understand better the passages in the Bible that speak of shepherds and their sheep. The sheep get to know the shepherd, because he spends the whole day with them in the field, and the shepherd, likewise, gets to know the sheep. And in the ancient Near East the shepherds also sometimes spent the nights with their sheep. Recall the announcement of the birth of Jesus in Luke's Gospel: "There were shepherds, living in the fields, keeping watch over their flock by night" (Luke 2:8

NRSV). The shepherd's life was closely bound up with his sheep. If one strayed, the shepherd went to look for it to bring it back, as we are shown by Jesus' story of the shepherd who left ninety-nine sheep to go in search of one.

The Bible uses the imagery of the shepherd often, probably because shepherding was such a common aspect of the culture of ancient Israel. God is often described as the shepherd of his people in the Old Testament. We all know the Twenty-Third Psalm, which begins, "The Lord is my shepherd . . ." In the Old Testament David is sometimes referred to as a shepherd of God's people. In the New Testament, the church office which often goes under the name of elder is defined as being the work of a shepherd.

In John's Gospel, Jesus refers to himself as "the good shepherd." One of the things a good shepherd did was protect his sheep. Jesus refers to himself as the good shepherd who lays down his life for his sheep. It would be in protecting the safety of his sheep that a shepherd would risk his life. Recall what young David related when he wanted to go out and fight Goliath, and everyone said, in effect, "You're just a kid. You are no match for this giant." Then David related some of his experiences as a shepherd boy. "Your servant used to keep sheep for his father," he said, "and whenever a lion or a bear came, and took a lamb from the flock, I went after it and struck it down, rescuing the lamb from its mouth; and if it turned against me, I would catch it by the jaw, strike it down, and kill it" (1 Sam 17:34–35 NRSV). Being a shepherd was not kid's stuff! A true shepherd risked his life on behalf of his sheep. They were that important to him.

The repetition of the laying down of his life theme later in this same paragraph shows that Jesus is referring ultimately to giving his life on the cross. His love and concern for his flock went that far. By comparing himself to a good shepherd here, Jesus assures us of his loving, redeeming care for us. We can put our trust in him to care for us, just as a sheep trusts its shepherd to protect and provide for it. It is this action of our good shepherd, Jesus, in laying down his life for his flock, that we remember and celebrate when we meet at this table each Lord's day.

30

The Table of Compassionate Giving (GK)

For many years our church, during February, joined hundreds of others in giving to meet crises of all kinds around the world—hunger, tsunamis, hurricanes, and others. The month climaxed with the "Week of Compassion" when we received an offering on the last Sunday. John 6:1–15 was sometimes used as a theme text. It records the story about Jesus feeding five thousand. This story must have spoken to deep needs among early Christians because it is the only miracle recorded in all four Gospels. Out in the wilderness, far from homes and sources of food, Jesus blessed five loaves and two fish and fed a huge crowd of hungry, needy people.

When Jesus told the disciples to feed them, they looked at the five loaves and two fish and asked, *What are these for so many people?* The need was so great, and their resources were so few, that they felt overwhelmed. Similar words are spoken in many places today. The countless numbers of hungry, homeless, and desperate people in this world overwhelms us. How can my small offering meet such a vast need?

Often, non-Christians also, simply out of human compassion, are motivated to feed the hungry. A story has circulated that gives the example of Tiger Woods. When he was four years old, he saw a TV program about hunger in Ethiopia. The pictures of children with extended bellies and the inability to swat flies off their faces moved him to ask his father if he could give his gold coin collection to help those children. His father took the coins but didn't tell Tiger that he sent the cash equivalent to a doctor friend in Ethiopia, intending to give the coins back to Tiger at an appropriate time.

As humans, we too feel the call to help our fellow human beings. But our motivation as Christians is even greater. We believe in a God who gave his only son. We believe in a Christ who gave his life. As Paul said, when some in the Corinthian church were questioning his sacrificial service on their behalf, "The love of Christ compels us, because we judge thus: that if one died for all, then all died; and He died for all that those who live should no longer live for themselves, but for Him who died for them and rose again" (2 Cor 5:14–15 NKJV).

Yes, we give because we are human, but also "the love of Christ compels us," and we know that he can bless our meager offering and use it to feed the world. He set the supreme example and we honor it each Sunday as we meet him at the table of compassionate giving.

31

Who Is Jesus Christ for You? (RH)

Mark's Gospel tells a fast-paced story of Jesus. The stories are short. The teachings are short. Over and over Mark says the people were amazed at Jesus. "We've never seen anything like this," they were saying. "We've never heard teaching like this before." He was moving around in Galilee. Every place he went he healed people, and they were amazed. When he taught in the synagogue at Capernaum the people "were astounded at his teaching." There in Capernaum he healed Peter's mother-in-law of a fever and word got out. At sundown the whole town gathered at his door, bringing him their sick and demon-possessed for healing. Then he left Capernaum and travelled in Galilee teaching and healing. When he returned to Capernaum some days later word got out that he was back, and people flocked to the house so that there was not even standing room around the door. And he taught them—and the crowd listened in amazement. When he walked down to the sea at Capernaum a large crowd gathered around him again to hear his teachings.

This is the way the story of Jesus goes in Mark's Gospel . . . until we get to chapter 6. Jesus goes to his hometown of Nazareth. He can work none of his mighty works there because his relatives and old neighbors see nothing special in him. Jesus' neighbors and relatives in Nazareth had no faith in him because *they thought they knew him.* He was the carpenter. They knew his mother—"Isn't this Mary's son?" They knew his brothers by name, and his sisters. All of Jesus' family lived there among them. He couldn't be anyone significant because he had lived just down the street. They knew Jesus. Or, so they thought. Therefore, Jesus could work none of his mighty works among them.

It wasn't that Jesus had no power to work his mighty works in Nazareth. The people of Nazareth had no expectations of Jesus. They dismissed him as the carpenter, Mary's son, the boy who grew up down the street. In Capernaum people crowded around the house where Jesus was so tightly that some men bringing a man to be healed had to go up on the roof and remove part of it to let the man down into the presence of Jesus. In the Decapolis on the other side of the Jordan, a deaf man was brought to Jesus and he healed him (Mark 5:31f). In Tyre, which was outside of Jewish territory, Jesus was eating at someone's home when a local woman interrupted the meal and begged Jesus to cast a demon out of her daughter, and he did (Mark 7:24); in Bethsaida people brought a blind man to Jesus and begged him to heal him, and he did (Mark 8:22). At Jericho a blind man named Bartimaeus cried out to Him, "Jesus, Son of David, have mercy on me." And he did (Mark 10:46ff).

But in Nazareth no one asked anything of Jesus. They didn't think he was anything more than the carpenter who used to have a shop down the street. So he left. He went to the surrounding villages and taught. And people continued to be amazed and healed. His fame continued to increase; but not in Nazareth. The people of Nazareth could not receive the Word of God because they thought that they knew who Jesus was. *But they didn't have a clue.*

I suspect that most of us in this room grew up with Jesus. We know who he is. We colored pictures of him in Sunday school classes when we were children. We sang songs about him. We heard stories about him. We know who Jesus is. But do we? As we come to this communion table and take into our bodies the elements that Jesus said were his body and blood, let us each ask ourselves, Do I really know him? Who is Jesus Christ *for me?*

Advent & Christmas

32

Advent: A Time to Prepare (GK)

The Advent season is here. The word "Advent" is from the Latin for "coming," and refers to the season of four Sundays before Christmas. It is a time of anticipation and preparation. The Christ is not yet born but he is coming soon and it's a time to get ready, to prepare for his coming.

A lot of preparation is needed when a baby is expected. Equipment and supplies must be purchased, perhaps a room redecorated, and other physical preparations made. More importantly, Mom and Dad need to prepare mentally and emotionally. Then, when the time is right, the baby comes.

It seems that even God prepared for the birth of his son. Paul says this about it: "But when the fullness of time had come, God sent his Son, born of a woman, born under the law, in order to redeem those who were under the law, so that we might receive adoption as children" (Gal 4:4–5 NRSV). The phrase, "in the fullness of time," or, in other words, when the time was right, implies a time of preparation.

God prepared the world for the birth of his son. He worked in history to bring about conditions that made it the right time for Christ to come. Politically, the Mediterranean world was united and at peace, thanks to the Roman Empire. One language, Greek, was spoken everywhere, making it possible to preach the gospel to many nations. The Romans built roads for their armies, which made it feasible for missionaries to travel. Also, the old gods had lost their power and attraction, leaving people hungry for a savior. It was the right time—the world was ready.

I wonder if God, the Father, also had to prepare himself? He knew what would happen; he knew how badly this sin-sick, Satan-enslaved world needed his Son. And he knew what it would cost to buy our freedom. Perhaps God was always ready, but I can't help feeling that the Father not only prepared the world but also prepared himself so that, when the time was right, "God sent his Son, born of a woman . . . so that we might receive adoption as children" (Gal 4:4–5 NRSV).

In this Advent season we can prepare for the coming of the Christ child by remembering why he came—to buy our freedom— and by remembering how much it cost. Therefore, we come to the table and recall how the Lord himself took the bread, broke it, and said, this is my body, given for you. And he took the cup also, saying, this cup is the new covenant in my blood poured out for the forgiveness of sins.

33

Peace Be with You (GK)

The Advent season has inspired many great hymns. A familiar one is "O Come, O Come, Emmanuel." The fourth stanza focuses on one of the important themes of the season, peace. It says: "O come Desire of nations, bind all peoples in one heart and mind. Bid envy, strife and quarrels cease; fill the whole world with heaven's peace."

When Isaiah spoke of the coming child he called him "Wonderful, Counselor, the mighty God, the everlasting Father, the Prince of Peace," and added, "Of the increase of his government and peace there will be no end" (Isa 9:6–7 NKJV).

The child, who became the man Jesus, met with his apostles for the last time in the upper room. There, according to John's Gospel, he spoke at length, preparing them for his departure. Several times he spoke about peace. For instance, he said, "Peace I leave with you; my peace I give to you. I do not give to you as the world gives" (John 14:27 NRSV). Near the end of his teaching he said, "I have said this to you, so that in me you may have peace" (John 16:33 NRSV).

He wanted them to have the gift of his peace. He said, "I do not give to you as the world gives." He, and they, knew all too well how the world gives peace. Their world was a Roman world. How did that world give peace? At the point of a sword and by crucifying anyone who was a threat to their rule of peace. The Pax Romana, the "Peace of Rome," was in force and Rome meant to keep it that way. Jesus saw firsthand how the world gives peace. As a boy he lived in the small village of Nazareth, close to the major city of Sephoris. A rebellion in Sephoris about the time when Jesus was born ended quickly with the death of some thirty thousand citizens, including two thousand who were crucified. Jesus would have learned that the cross was the symbol of how the world gives peace.

Jesus said he wanted to give them *his* peace. Amazingly, the cross became his symbol of peace. In Romans 5 Paul points out that it was through death on the cross that Christ reconciled us to God, thus making peace. And as for the hostilities and divisions we experience in the world, Paul explains in Ephesians 2 that Jesus put these to death through the cross as well. The symbolism of the cross was transformed when Jesus was crucified.

There is a beautiful verse in Psalm 85 that, I think, summarizes the symbolism of the cross for us: "Steadfast love and faithfulness will meet; righteousness and peace will kiss each other" (Ps 85:10 NRSV). As we take communion may the cross be both righteousness and peace for us.

34

"Yet, I will rejoice" (RH)

The year 2020 was an unusual year, to put it in perhaps the best light possible. For some it was a devastating year. It was a difficult year for our congregation. The fourth-century African Christian bishop Augustine once said that our greatest reward as Christians is to enjoy God and that "all of us who enjoy Him may enjoy one another in Him."[1] We who are a part of this congregation do "enjoy one another" in God, but that was hard to do in 2020 when we were unable to assemble for our weekly worship and fellowship. We were not able properly to weep with those who weep or to rejoice with those who rejoice. Our church family lost a mother in 2020, and a young daughter. But we were not able to weep together or comfort one another. And there were two weddings in our church family, but we were not able to rejoice with those who rejoice as we normally would. And then we approached what is traditionally one of the happiest days in the year, a time when families and friends get together to celebrate the birth of Jesus and enjoy one another's company. But in 2020 such gatherings posed the possibility of adding to the mounting threat of spreading a deadly virus.

While the details of his situation were completely different from ours, I want to suggest that the prophet Habakkuk had something to say that is worth thinking about as we prepare to participate

---

1. Augustine, *On Christian Doctrine*, 1.35.

in the Lord's Supper on this fourth Sunday of Advent in 2020. Habakkuk is one of my favorite prophets. It's a little book—three chapters that you can read in ten minutes. That's why he is called a "minor" prophet. The adjective "minor" applied to a group of prophetic writings in the Old Testament is not a value judgment on the worth of what they say. It means simply that the minor prophets wrote small books compared to the large books of Isaiah, Jeremiah, and Ezekiel, the so-called major prophets.

The book of Habakkuk begins with a strong complaint to God and ends with one of the most powerful and beautiful expressions of faith that you can find in the Bible. The entire book is a kind of dialogue between the prophet and God. Habakkuk starts the dialogue by crying out in prayer, "O Lord, how long shall I cry for help, and you will not listen?" (Hab 1:2 NRSV). Did you ever feel like that? That your prayers don't get beyond the ceiling of the room where you are praying? Habakkuk did. He had been praying about the evil in his nation and God apparently wasn't doing anything about it. Habakkuk saw the violence and lack of justice among his people, but his prayers didn't seem to alter anything.

Then God responds in the dialogue and says in effect: You are going to be amazed at what I am preparing for your nation. I am bringing the most powerful, fearful nation in the world down on your little nation as punishment for all its wrongdoing. They will come like the wind with their destructive power. This was not the answer the prophet wanted! His first response was to object, with something like, "But Lord, those people are worse than we are!" The dialogue continues and includes some of the most beautiful and best known verses in the Bible: "The righteous live by their faith"; "The earth will be filled with the knowledge of the glory of the Lord, as the waters cover the sea," and, "The Lord is in his holy temple; let all the earth keep silence before him" (Hab 2:4, 14, 20 NRSV).

Finally the little book ends with another prayer by Habbakuk, but this one is offered in an entirely different spirit than the one with which he began his book. It is the final words of that closing prayer of Habakkuk that speak with power to our situation. "Though the fig tree does not blossom, and no fruit is on the vines; though the produce of the olive fails and the fields yield no food; though the flock is cut off from the fold and there is no herd in the stalls, yet I will rejoice in the Lord; I will exult in the God of my salvation" (Hab 3:17–18 NRSV). The prophet has come to realize that his source of joy is not the circumstances of his life, but his God who gives him salvation.

This kind of joy is what we Christians celebrate at this season of the year as we focus our attention on the fact that the "Emmanuel, which means God is with us," who was promised by Isaiah (Matt 1:23 NRSV), has come. *He is the God of our salvation.* And this is the joy that we celebrate each Sunday when we partake of the Lord's Supper. Emmanuel has come. "I will exult in the God of my salvation."

35

Advent (RH)

Advent is a Latin word meaning "coming" or "presence." We use the word of the season approaching Christmas because we are celebrating the coming of Christ to redeem the world. We spend a lot of money to buy gifts for people at Christmas time. Merchants promote the Christmas season to push their annual sales into the black. We eat a lot. Perhaps we party a lot. Then Christmas is over and everything returns to the way it was before.

The third-century Christian scholar named Origen asked a pertinent question about Advent in a sermon he preached in Caesarea, Palestine in the third century AD. "What advantage is it," he asked, "if I should say that Jesus has come only in that flesh which he received from Mary, and I do not also show that he has come in this flesh of mine?"[1]

What would it mean for Jesus to come "in this flesh of mine"? Origen cited three verses from Paul that show what he understood it to mean. The first was Romans 6:19: "Just as you used to present the members of your body to serve injustice . . . so now offer them to serve justice." The second was Galatians 2:19–20: "I have been crucified with Christ and I no longer live, but Christ lives in me." And the third was Romans 8:35: "Who shall separate us from the

1. Origen, *Homilies*, 101 (modified).

love of God which is in Christ Jesus? Shall tribulation, or distress, or danger, or the sword?" (My translations of Origen's texts.)

The first of these verses points to a moral indicator of the presence of Christ in our lives—justice in our dealings with all people. The second refers to a Christ-controlled life in which doing what he wants is more important than doing what I want, and the third points to a firm confidence in God's love for us displayed in Christ, a love that overcomes the fear of the calamities and disasters that confront us in life, whether they are external or internal.

One of the important meanings of Advent is to let Christ work redemptively right now in my life.

> O holy Child of Bethlehem!
> Descend to us we pray;
> Cast out our sin and enter in,
> Be born in us today.[2]

As we come to the Lord's Table on this final Sunday of Advent may we open our lives afresh to the coming of Christ *in us*.

2. Phillips Brooks, "O Little Town of Bethlehem."

36

The Birth of the Light (RH)

"In the beginning was the Word, and the Word was with God, and the Word was God. He was in the beginning with God. All things came into existence through him, and without him not one thing came into existence. What came into existence in him was life, and the life was the light of human beings. And the light shines in the darkness, and the darkness has not overcome it. . . . And the Word became flesh and lived among us, and we beheld his glory . . ." (John 1:1–5, 14, my translation.)

This is the way John introduces his story of Jesus. There is no birth of Jesus narrative in John's Gospel. There are no shepherds, no magi, no angels, no Bethlehem, no citations of Old Testament prophecies about the coming of the Messiah. John's story of Jesus is rooted in the creation narrative, in the opening words of the Bible. "In the beginning God made heaven and earth. . . . And darkness was over the abyss. . . . And God said, Let light come into existence. And light came into existence . . ." (Gen 1:1–3, my translation).

In the opening words of his Gospel, John identifies the Word with "the light of human beings," intentionally, I think, relating his opening words to the opening words of Genesis about the darkness and the coming of light. This is the Word that John says a few sentences later "became flesh" and lived among us. Jesus as the light of humanity is an important theme in John's Gospel. Three times in chapters 8–12 Jesus says, "I am the light of the world." In 8:12 Jesus says, "I am the light of the world; the one who follows me will not walk in darkness, but will have the light of life" (my translation).

The light he is speaking of, of course, is not the kind the sun produces—or that our modern light bulbs produce. Light and darkness are used symbolically. He is talking about the enlightenment of our minds—our inner being—that results from knowing and following Christ. In a commentary written in the early third century of the Christian era, a Christian named Origen said of the light and darkness John speaks of, "This light . . . 'shines in the darkness' of our souls. It has come to stay where the world rulers of this darkness [mentioned by Paul] live. . . . This light shines in the darkness and is pursued by it, but it is not overcome."[1]

The coming of Christ was seen as light, not just in John's Gospel, but throughout the Bible. Luke tells the story of the aged saint named Simeon who had been promised that he would see the Messiah before he died. When Mary and Joseph took the infant Jesus to the temple for purification in accordance with the Mosaic law, Simeon was there. He took the baby in his arms and said, "Master, now you are dismissing your servant in peace, . . . for my eyes have seen your salvation . . . a *light* for revelation to the Gentiles and for glory to your people Israel" (Luke 2:29, 30, 32 NRSV, my emphasis). In 1868 Phillips Brooks wrote in his well-known Christmas carol "O Little Town of Bethlehem":

> Yet in thy dark streets shineth
> The everlasting Light.

Christmas is a celebration of the coming of the light of God to the dark world of human sin and fear. The beginning and the end of this coming are tied closely together. The Christ who came into the world as light was arrested and condemned for the sins of the world in the darkness. In that last dark night the Light took bread and blessed it and gave it to his disciples and said, "Take, eat; this is my body. Then he took a cup, and after giving thanks he gave it to them, saying, Drink from it, all of you; for this is my blood of the covenant, which is poured out for many for the forgiveness of sins" (Matt 26:26–28 NRSV).

1. Origen, *Commentary on John: Books 1–10*, 139.

37

Mary, Did You Know? (RH)

In the first chapter of Luke's Gospel we are told that the angel Gabriel was sent by God to a virgin named Mary, who was promised in marriage to a man named Joseph, whose family was descended from David (Luke 1:26–27).

Mary was probably a teenager when the angel Gabriel came to her. Luke says she was "promised in marriage." This was something more formal and legally binding than what we know today as "engaged." It involved the two families as much as the two people who would eventually marry. The normal age for promising a girl in marriage in that culture was twelve to thirteen years of age. In the late twentieth century the musical group Pentatonix made popular a song with the title, "Mary, Did You Know?"

That is an interesting question. Mary, did you know? Did you know that the words the angel Gabriel spoke to you about the child you would bear echoed the words of the ancient Hebrew prophet Nathan to King David when he spoke of David's death and said to David in the name of God, "I will raise up your offspring after you, . . . and I will establish the throne of his kingdom forever. I will be a father to him and he shall be a son to me" (2 Sam 7:12–14 NRSV).

Mary, did you know that the angel Gabriel who spoke to you appears only twice in your ancient Hebrew Scriptures, both times in the book of Daniel where he comes as a messenger of hope to announce that the oppression of God's people is near its end (Dan

8:16; 9:21)? Mary may have known more than we might want to give her credit for at first sight. If we take into account the song that Luke puts in her mouth a little later in the first chapter of his Gospel, a song we call the Magnificat, she concludes that song by referring to God remembering "the promise he made to our ancestors, to Abraham and to his descendants forever" (Luke 1:55 NRSV).

Mary, did you know? I think she certainly did not know the depths she would be plunged into as mother of the Messiah. When Jesus was about a month old Mary and Joseph took him to the temple for some customary purification offerings. An old saint of Israel named Simeon took the baby in his arms. The words he spoke to Mary hinted at the tragic side to being the mother of the Messiah. He identified her baby boy as God's salvation and a light to the Gentiles. That was a radical assertion, for God's salvation, up to this point, had been the unique privilege of the Jewish people. And then Simeon spoke an ominous, enigmatic, prophetic word to Mary about what lay ahead: "This child is destined," he said, "for the falling and rising of many in Israel, and to be a sign that will be opposed." And then he said directly to Mary, "And a sword will pierce your own soul too" (Luke 2:34 NRSV). It was that sword, I think, that Mary did not at this point understand, or if she did, she must have deeply dreaded.

Mary, did you know that when your baby was still a toddler you would have to take him and flee from your homeland and live for several years as an immigrant in a foreign land because the irrational head of state named Herod was afraid of him and had set in motion a massacre of infants in the region of Bethlehem in an attempt to kill him?

Mary, did you know how your Son's part in God's plan for human salvation was going to play out? Did you know the pain you would feel in about thirty years when you would stand griefstricken at the foot of a Roman cross that held your son, rejected, accused, and condemned by the leaders of your religion, sentenced to death by the local governing authority, and forsaken, it seemed, even by God. Mary, did you know?

Mary, did you know that more than two thousand years after the birth of your son millions of people would stop the normal activities of their lives to celebrate his birth, and that week after week people around the world would gather regularly to remember his life, his death, and his resurrection at this table? Mary, did you know?

96

38

Bethlehem (RH)

O little town of Bethlehem
How still we see thee lie.

Phillips Brooks, a pastor in Philadelphia, wrote the words of this favorite Christmas carol in 1868 following a pilgrimage to the Holy Land. He was inspired by the view of Bethlehem from the hills of Palestine at nighttime. It was a peaceful scene.

Bethlehem is one of the oldest towns in the world. It is first mentioned in Genesis (35:19). But it is not mentioned there in connection with joy or celebration. It is mentioned in connection with death. Jacob's wife Rachel died giving birth to their twelfth son. Jacob buried her, it says, on the road to Bethlehem (Gen 35:19; 48:7).

Bethlehem is next mentioned in the book of Judges, where it is connected with violence, some of it quite gruesome (Judg 12 and 18–19). Bethlehem and its environs was certainly not always the peaceful scene that Philips Brooks imagined in the mid-nineteenth century.

Bethlehem has an important place in the book of Ruth, though it has its own tragedies and sorrows even there. Naomi, Ruth's mother-in-law, was from Bethlehem. Naomi and her family had migrated to Moab because of famine in the region of Bethlehem. There her two sons had married, and then subsequently died, as did Naomi's own husband. Ruth, one of the Moabite women who had married a son of Naomi, returned to Bethlehem with her. Naomi went back to Bethlehem a bitter woman because of all she had lost in Moab. Ruth married Boaz, a local man in Bethlehem, and they later had a son they named Obed. Obed became the grandfather of King David. This is the beginning of the association of Bethlehem with David in the Bible, a theme so important in the birth narratives of Jesus in the New Testament.

The first time hope is associated with Bethlehem in the Bible is in the famous prophetic statement made in Micah 5:2 (NRSV): "But you, O Bethlehem of Ephrathah, who are one of the little clans of Judah, from you shall come forth for me one who is to rule in Israel, whose origin is from of old, from ancient days." The Jews, as Matthew 2:3–6 shows, understood this to be a prophecy about the birth of the Messiah. When the magi from the east, who had been following a star, asked in Jerusalem where the new king of the Jews had just been born, the chief priests and scribes directed them to Bethlehem on the basis of the words of Micah 5:2.

Luke emphasizes the connection of Bethlehem with David and of Jesus' family with David. Jesus was born in Bethlehem because there was a Roman tax census that demanded that every head of family register in the city or town from which he descended. Luke says that Joseph took Mary and went "to the city of David called Bethlehem, because he was descended from the house and family of David" (Luke 2:4 NRSV). From you, Bethlehem, "shall come forth . . . the one . . . whose origin is from of old, from ancient days."

And so Jesus, the Christ child, was born in Bethlehem of Judea. But the ancient human violence, tragedy, and death connected with Bethlehem also continue. For Matthew says that "When Herod saw that he had been tricked by the wise men, he was infuriated, and he sent and killed all the children in and around Bethlehem who were two years old or under. . . . Then was fulfilled what had been spoken through the prophet Jeremiah: 'A voice was heard in Ramah, wailing and loud lamentation, Rachel'"—remember Rachel and the first mention of Bethlehem in the Bible—Rachel "weeping for her children; she refused to be consoled, because they are no more" (Matt 2:16–18 NRSV). Some of the most important

doctrines concerning the deepest mysteries of the Christian faith
are associated with this little town.

> O little town of Bethlehem
> How still we see thee lie
> Above thy deep and dreamless sleep
> The silent stars go by
> Yet in thy dark streets shineth
> The everlasting Light
> The hopes and fears of all the years
> Are met in thee tonight.

39

The Cradle and the Cross (GK)

I know that we like having a Christmas of lights and songs, of rejoicing and praising, but the communion table reminds us that pain is also involved. It reminds us that Jesus was born to die. It reminds us that the cradle in a stable is joined by the cross on a hill as symbols of who Jesus was and why he came. They can never be separated. They remind us that joy and pain are never far apart.

We realize this when we read all of Luke's account of Jesus' birth and infancy. In the first two chapters of Luke, we see the beautiful story of Jesus' birth—Mary's song, his birth in a manger, angels singing, and shepherds praising. But then Luke tells us a story that foreshadows the pain and suffering of the cross, not just to Jesus, but also to his mother, Mary.

Shortly after Jesus was born Mary and Joseph took him to the temple to "present Him to the Lord," since the law stated that every firstborn male belonged to the Lord. There they came across an old man named Simeon, who had been told by the Holy Spirit that he would not die until he saw the Lord's Messiah. When he saw Jesus, Simeon took him in his arms, raised his eyes to heaven, and declared, "My eyes have seen Your salvation." But when he handed Jesus back to Mary he said, "This child is appointed for the fall and rise of many in Israel, and for a sign to be opposed—and a sword will pierce even your own soul" (Luke 2:34–35 NAS).

John Killinger, pastor and professor of preaching, tells how those words were driven into his soul. He and his family were in Spain, in a museum, standing before one of the great Spanish crucifixion scenes. The painting, like so many Spanish works of art, was dark and brooding, unlike the sunlit plains of Spain. Christ hung on the cross. In the lower foreground a woman knelt. "Who is that" asked Killinger's six-year-old. "That's Mary, Jesus' mother," he explained. The child was quiet for a second or two and then said, very solemnly, "That must have hurted her." Since then, Killinger says, "I have not been able to read Simeon's words to Mary, 'a sword will pierce through your own soul also,' without remembering that observation."[1]

Luke has forever linked the baby born in a manger with the image of a cross on a hill and the pain and suffering it brought to Mary. Jesus was born to die. The cradle and the cross cannot be separated. At this table, as we remember how Jesus suffered on our behalf, may we also remember Mary, and many others, even today, who know him as friend, as teacher, and as Lord, and who, in some way, enter into his sufferings.

1. Killinger, *Fundamentals*, 121.

Lent, Easter, & Pentecost

40

The Wounded Healer (GK)

The TV show Sixty Minutes played a report after the mass shootings in El Paso, Texas and Dayton, Ohio which focused on a couple whose daughter was killed in the Colorado Theater shooting several years ago. This couple who understood what it meant to lose a loved one to gun violence began going to the sites of mass shootings and offering their understanding, compassion, and support to those whose loved ones had been killed. Often, it is those who have suffered who can help the most because they know how others feel. They become what Henri Nouwen called "wounded healers."

The experience of Helmut Thielicke makes clear how "wounded healers" can provide what we really need. Helmut Thielicke was a German theologian and pastor who preached in the Stuttgart Cathedral during World War II. The Allies made Stuttgart a major target and bombed it mercilessly and repeatedly. The cathedral was destroyed and then Thielicke's home was destroyed. He went to a village nearby that had not been bombed, hoping to find a house for his family. There he had a peculiar experience. As he walked through the village, he remembered how he had tried in his mind to escape the sight of bombed-out ruins and suffering people by imagining that he lived in a quiet village where neighbors sat on their porches greeting passersby with warmth and friendliness. By this he hoped to find peace in his heart. But as he walked through the village, he did not find peace. Instead, the idyllic scene was tormenting rather than tranquilizing. He said, "It drove me back to the ruined city and the people whose faces were still marked by the ruins of terror. There I felt at home. They understood what I had gone through because they had suffered it themselves. There is nothing more comforting than to have people who understand one."[1] They were his wounded healers.

In our struggles, when we are tested and fail, when we are in a war, as Paul says in Ephesians, "against principalities, against powers, against the rulers of the darkness of this age, against spiritual hosts of wickedness" (Eph 6:12 NRSV), we too have a "wounded healer." He is our commander in chief, but he does not sit in a heavenly office sending out commands and comforting messages. He is in the trenches with us. Hebrews 2:18 (NRSV) says, "Because he himself was tested by what he suffered, he is able to help those who are being tested." He knows what it is like.

The prophet Isaiah described our wounded healer this way: "He was wounded for our transgressions, he was bruised for our iniquities; the chastisement of our peace was upon him, and with his stripes we are healed" (Isa 53:5 NKJV).

In the upper room Jesus pointed to himself as our wounded healer when he took the bread and blessed it, broke it, gave it to them, and said, *take, eat, this is my body,* and the cup, saying, *this is my blood of the new covenant, which is shed for many for the remission of sins* (Matt 26:26–28 NKJV).

---

1. Thielicke, *Christ,* 16–17.

41

"I have been crucified" (GK)

As though he himself were present and had experienced it himself, Paul said, "I have been crucified with Christ; and it is no longer I who live but it is Christ who lives in me" (Gal 2:19b–20a NRSV). How could that be? Can we enter another person's experience so completely that it becomes our experience too?

Don't we do this sometimes through stories? It's possible to get into a good story so much that you identify with and feel with the person you are reading about. You feel their fear, their joy, or their frustration. A friend explained how this happens to him as a Civil War reenactor: "When we put on old clothes, military or civilian, and start acting and talking like they did in the 1860s, we become that which we portray."

He went on to speak of what he called "magic moments, when sometimes, even for a brief instant, it is like we are transported back 150 years. And it can be the simplest thing—the smell of gunpowder, roasting coffee beans over the fire, or whatever. One of my first magic moments took place following an officer's mess. One of our captains took out a cigar, bit off the end, and spit it onto the ground before lighting up. People don't do that anymore. For a brief moment, it was 1863."

An Israeli tour guide demonstrated how the story of his people affected him. Our tour group was traveling from Jerusalem to Tel Aviv by bus when he pointed to some low hills and began telling the story of a battle that took place there. It sounded like he had been in it. He told it with precise details, and I wondered if it was during the war of 1967. No, he said, and he named a battle that took place before the time of Christ. But it was his people, his story, and he experienced it. History had become like firsthand memory for him.

The Jewish Passover meal, even today, combines the story of the exodus with the action of eating certain foods to help Jewish people live again their escape from Egypt and their rescue by God. It is a kind of reenactment that brings the ancient experience into their lives today.

Likewise, Jesus gave us both a story and actions that help us experience what he did for us. "Do this," he said. "Take, eat," he said; "drink," he said. These are action words. And he said as you do it "remember me." By our actions and by remembering and telling the story we enter his experience, and he enters into our lives. That's why Paul went on to say in Galatians 2, "The life I now live in the flesh I live by faith in the Son of God, who loved me and gave himself for me" (Gal 2:20b NRSV). May we also come to the cross at the table and say with Paul, "I have been crucified with Christ; and it is no longer I who live but it is Christ who lives in me."

42

The Cross and the Tree of Life (RH)

The cross of Christ stands at the center of all early Christian preaching and teaching. The apostle Paul had placed it there when he asserted, in one of the earliest Christian writings that we possess, that "the message about the cross is foolishness to those who are perishing, but to us who are being saved it is the power of God"(1 Cor 1:18 NRSV).

It is the cross of Christ that we celebrate in the Lord's Supper. We usually think about the pain and the shame of crucifixion, and both of those were certainly involved. It was an excruciating way to be put to death; it was reserved for slaves and the worst kinds of criminals. The Roman lawyer Cicero prosecuted and won a conviction against a Roman provincial governor named Verres in 70 BC for, among other things, crucifying Roman citizens during his governorship of Sicily. It was illegal to crucify Roman citizens. Crucifixion was a slave's death.

It was especially difficult for Jews to associate Jesus with the work of God because of the crucifixion. They looked at the crucifixion in connection with their law in Deuteronomy 21:23 (NRSV), which says that "anyone hung on a tree is under God's curse," and they considered being hung on a wooden cross to fall under that law, and Jesus, consequently, to have been cursed by God.

The early Christians, however, took that reference to being hanged on a tree and transformed it from being a reference to death to a reference to the life that comes through Christ as the result of his crucifixion. They began to connect the "tree" on which Christ was crucified with the "tree of life" which stood in the garden of Eden in Genesis 3, and which is said to stand in the new Jerusalem in Revelation 22.

In the very early second century we have letters from a Christian bishop of Antioch named Ignatius. In one of his letters Ignatius refers to Christians as "fruit of the cross" and in another he refers to Christians as "branches of the cross."[1] Both of those images suggest that Ignatius was thinking of the cross of Christ as a "tree," but not a tree that produces death, rather a tree that produces life. It appears that quite early Christians associated the tree of life mentioned in Genesis 2 with the cross on which Christ died, and identified themselves as the branches or fruit of that cross. By doing this, the tree thought by Jews to place the death of Christ under a curse, or the cross which made his death a scandal among Romans, was transformed from a tree of shame and death to a tree of hope and life.

When we celebrate the Lord's Supper, which is centered in the cross of Christ, we are not celebrating his death; we are celebrating his life—resurrection life.

1. *Apostolic Fathers*, 249, 221.

43

"Remember Jesus Christ, raised from the dead" (RH)

"Remember Jesus Christ, raised from the dead." Those are the words of the apostle Paul in 2 Timothy 2:8 (NRSV). Paul was an old man when he said that. He was in prison, expecting, probably correctly, that before long he would be executed for his preaching of Christ. He says later in the letter, "The time of my departure has come. I have fought the good fight, I have finished the race, I have kept the faith" (2 Tim 4:6–7 NRSV). His eyes are fixed, not on further work or relaxation on this earth, but on the reward that he will receive from the Lord following his death.

But he had this young protégé named Timothy whom he had earlier taken under his wings as a co-worker in his mission work. Timothy had a special place in Paul's heart. Paul may have baptized him. He certainly knew Timothy's mother and grandmother, Eunice and Lois. He calls Timothy his "beloved child" in the addresses of his two letters to Timothy, and refers to him as "my child" when he addresses him directly in the letter.

But now he is writing his last letter to Timothy. "Remember Jesus Christ, raised from the dead, a descendant of David—that is my gospel," Paul says. What a simple, profound statement Paul sums up the gospel in: "Jesus Christ, raised from the dead." That's the good news, Timothy: "Jesus Christ, raised from the dead." Remember that.

But it's easy to forget, isn't it? We forget all kinds of things: appointments—we have to write them down either electronically or on paper—birthdays, maybe anniversaries (especially husbands!), we just forget in the mix of all the things in which we get involved. And we forget the truly good news: "Jesus Christ, raised from the dead."

We need reminders. That's why the church gathers regularly at this table. Jesus knew that we need memory joggers. The Lord's Supper is about remembering. It's about remembering the gospel: "Jesus Christ, raised from the dead." When Jesus first introduced this practice to his disciples on the night before he was crucified, he said, "Do this in remembrance of me" (1 Cor 11:24–25 NRSV). And from that night to this day, the church has continued each week to "remember Jesus Christ, raised from the dead" at this table.

44

To Life! (GK)

When I open Facebook, it always asks, "What's on your mind, George?" I was tempted recently to answer with one word, "Death," to see what the response would be. It's true, however, that I think of death rather often, for several reasons. One, because it's in the news—graphically and repeatedly. I should stop watching the news, but I won't. I am reminded of death also because of my age. The longer I live the more friends and family members I lose. Another reason I think of death is that both my daughter and my wife have had near-death experiences. One doesn't forget things like that.

My reading also leads me to think about death. Some books I read are mysteries, which always focus on someone's death. A book that I reread occasionally is not a mystery, but it often speaks of death. It was written by Rachel Naomi Remen, MD, who works with cancer patients. One of them had survived three major surgeries in only five months. He described himself to her afterwards as "born again." She asked him what he meant, and he said the experience of facing his death had challenged his ideas about life. He was stripped of all that he knew, the ideologies and philosophies that he had built his life on, and was "left only with the unshakeable conviction that life itself was holy." She commented, "He had discovered that we live not by choice but by grace. And that life itself is a blessing."[1]

---

1. Remen, *My Grandfather's Blessings,* 325.

It occurred to me that Jesus must have thought something like this when he faced death during his ministry. He knew that he would die but not for a Pharisaic ideology—or for any other ideology people build their lives on—and certainly not any of the polarizing "isms" that divide us today. He was very clear about why he came, which was also why he had to die. He said plainly in John 10:10–11 (NRSV), "I came that they may have life, and have it abundantly. I am the good shepherd; the good shepherd lays down his life for the sheep." When we read through John's Gospel, we find repeatedly that it's all about life. He opens by saying, "In the beginning was the Word and the Word was with God and the Word was God," and quickly adds, "In him was life and the life was the light of all people" (John 1:1, 4 NRSV). And he continues throughout the Gospel to show us the one who said, "I am the way the truth and the life," and "I am the resurrection and the life" (John 14:6; 11:25 NRSV).

The cancer patient was right. Life is holy, and it is ours by grace. This broken bread and the cup remind us of the life Jesus gave that we might live. It would be appropriate when we lift the cup to use the traditional Jewish toast that says simply, "To Life!"

45

Sophocles and Paul (RH)

I did much of my graduate work in the obscure field of Greek and Latin studies called classics. In that program I had to read a lot of ancient Greek and Latin literature. One of the Greek plays that I studied was Sophocles's tragedy *Antigone,* which was the name of the heroine, if you can call her that. I recently reread *Antigone*—in English this time, not Greek—it goes much faster!

In one of the choruses Sophocles praises the ingenuity and accomplishments of humanity. He begins by saying, "The world is full of marvelous things, but nothing is more marvelous than a human being." Then he lists what he considers to be the outstanding human accomplishments in the Greek world of the fifth century BC. Human beings have conquered the sea with their boats; they have learned how to use the storm winds to drive their boats; with their horse- or oxen-drawn plows they have learned how to turn the soil so that the earth produces food for them; they can trap birds, beasts, and the fish of the sea in their nets; they have tamed the horse and the wild bull and made them their servants. They have developed a language so they can speak; they can think; they can create a state. They know how to build houses to protect themselves from the cold and the rain. There is nothing that they cannot provide for themselves. But, Sophocles ends that chorus praising the accomplishments of humanity with the conclusion that humanity has been unable to devise any escape from death (*Antigone* 332–61).

This was the dismal conclusion that Sophocles pronounced on his happy description of the inventiveness of human beings in the fifth century BC. They have found no escape from death.

About five and a half centuries after Sophocles, in the middle of the first century AD, the apostle Paul fairly shouts out in jubilation, "Death has been swallowed up in victory. Where, O death, is your victory? Where, O death, is your sting?" (1 Cor 15:54–55 NRSV). Instead of the invulnerable conqueror of every single human being that Sophocles saw in death, Paul saw a vanquished enemy whose power and rule had been broken. What had happened in that lapse of time between Sophocles and Paul to give Paul such a radically different view of death? The resurrection of Jesus of Nazareth had happened.

The church celebrates the resurrection of Jesus every Sunday in every act of worship, but especially when we partake of the Lord's Supper. Ignatius, a Christian bishop in the early second century, referred to the Lord's Supper as "the medicine of immortality."[1] What a difference Jesus has made to the hopes of humanity!

1. *Apostolic Fathers*, 199.

46

The Cross as Center (RH)

The story of the Hebrew prophet Elijah is told in the final chapters of 1 Kings and the opening chapters of 2 Kings. Elijah was a very influential prophet, though he never wrote a book as many later prophets did. Probably the most famous story of Elijah is that of his contest with the prophets of Baal, when he called out to God and God sent fire from heaven and consumed Elijah's offering and altar on Mount Carmel. Then Elijah, elated by God's show of force, slaughtered 450 prophets of Baal in his attempt to rid Israel of Baal worship. But things backfired for the prophet when Queen Jezebel, a devotee of Baal worship, heard about the slaughter and vowed to see Elijah himself killed. Elijah fled for his life for forty days and nights, until he came to Mt. Horeb and hid in a cave on the mountain. God came to speak to him there.

It's the story of the way God revealed himself to the prophet on the mountain that I want you to think about. It's an interesting description. Elijah is hiding in his cave and he hears this terrible wind, so strong it was shattering rocks. It must have been something like a tornado. Elijah must have thought, "That display of power must be God." But the writer says, "The Lord was not in the wind." After the wind there was an earthquake. Elijah must have thought, that is surely God, but again the writer says, "The Lord was not in the earthquake." After the earthquake came a fire, perhaps something like a forest fire, but again, "the Lord was not in the fire." Then, as the NRSV translates it, there was "a sound of sheer silence" (see 1 Kgs 19:11–13).

We don't get to hear that sound very often in our world of constant noises. Several summers ago my wife and I were in the Crooked River Gorge near Prineville, Oregon. We hiked up to a place called Chimney Rock. It was a lot longer hike than what the sign had promised and it was a very isolated area! It was a hot day and the path led steadily uphill. We both noticed as we were standing in the shade of one of the scrubby little trees along the way that there was absolute silence—no sound of birds, animals, human voices, motors, airplanes, the whine of car tires on asphalt—no sound at all. That's what Elijah heard, and that's when God spoke.

Now shift from Elijah to Jesus. What a disappointment he was to most of the Hebrew people of his day. They wanted wind, earthquake, and fire from the Messiah—shake those occupying Romans, burn down their camps, and blow down their walls like the big bad wolf. Let them know that there's a God in heaven who looks after his people. But that wasn't how God revealed himself. The Jewish aristocracy, in league with the Romans, prevailed against Jesus, and God didn't raise a finger to stop them. The mighty Messiah the majority had been hoping for was crucified with two common criminals—without even offering a fight. What a disappointment, and how difficult it was to hear God speaking in the crucifixion.

Martin Luther once called the crucifixion the backside of God, like what Moses got to see when God put him in the cleft in the rock. You could easily miss seeing God at work in the crucifixion of Jesus. There wasn't anything there that looked holy or glorious, or was suggestive of God in any way. "My God, my God, why have you forsaken me?" (Mark 15:34 NRSV), Jesus called out from the cross. Paul reminds us in 1 Corinthians 1 that in the cross God was making a mockery of human wisdom and power, revealing himself in a scene of foolishness and weakness. Human wisdom says, "There is no way the almighty God would reveal himself like that." But that is where and how God chose to speak his most powerful message to humanity. If you want to know me, he says, then you must come to the cross. You either find me here, or you won't find me.

The Lord's Supper invites us to the cross of Christ. This is what Jesus was pointing to when he took bread and broke it and gave it to the disciples and said, "Take, eat, This is my body." He meant his body offered on the cross. When he gave them the cup and said, "This is my blood of the covenant which is poured out for many for the forgiveness of sins" (Matt 26:26, 28 NRSV), he was pointing them to the blood he would shed the next afternoon on the cross. The Lord's Supper directs our thoughts to the central revelation God has given us of himself—the cross of Jesus our Lord.

47

A Thing of Beauty (GK)

There was nothing beautiful about a Roman cross. It was made of rough lumber, a simple cross beam, either at the top or nailed on part way down. Some crosses had a protruding piece at the bottom where the victim could rest his feet. Crosses were not attractive things that you would use to decorate your house. Nor was the person hanging there a thing of beauty. A beaten, bloody body is not a pleasant sight. In a prophetic word about the suffering servant Isaiah said, "There is no beauty that we should desire him" (Isa 53:2 NKJV).

But today the cross is used as a thing of beauty. I Googled "Roman cross" on the internet but what I found looked too nice. We use precious metals to make it into jewelry to adorn our bodies, or we use fine lumber and make beautiful replicas to decorate our churches.

For a long time, this struck me as ironic. Picturing or thinking of the cross as beautiful surely must be misleading. How can a cruel and ugly instrument of execution be turned into a thing of beauty? How can we do such a thing?

Well, we can't—but God can. He transformed it by placing Jesus upon it. In his book *Beauty Will Save the World,* Brian Zahnd points out: "The unique form of Christianity is the cruciform—Christ upon the cross, arms outstretched in offered embrace, forgiving the world of its sins. This is the beauty that saves the world, and the symbol of this saving grace is the cross." He goes on to say: "That the Roman cross, an instrument of physical torture and psychological terror, could ever become an object of beauty representing faith, hope, and love is an amazing miracle of transformation. Every cross adorning a church is in itself a sermon—a sermon proclaiming that if Christ can transform the Roman instrument of execution into a thing of beauty, there is hope that in Christ all things can be made beautiful."[1]

However, it must be added that to see the beauty of the cross in all its glory, as with many beautiful images, you must stand in the right place. It must be viewed from this side of the resurrection and in faith. It must be seen through the prism of the resurrection. From that perspective we join the hymn writer to say:

> In the old rugged cross, stained with blood so divine,
> A wondrous beauty I see.
> For twas on that old cross Jesus suffered and died
> To pardon and sanctify me.

As we see him on the cross let us also hear his words spoken at the Last Supper. Of the bread which he broke and gave to them: "This is my body, given for you;" and of the cup, "this . . . is the new covenant in my blood" (Luke 22:19–20 NRSV). How beautiful is that?!

---

1. Zahnd, *Beauty,* 60.

48

It's Not Over! (GK)

As I read Psalm 31 a line in it took me to Jesus on the cross. In verse 5 (NRSV) the psalmist says, "Into your hand I commit my spirit." These were Jesus' last words, according to Luke's Gospel (23:46), uttered shortly before he died. When I picture Jesus on the cross and hear these words they sound like the last gasp of a dying man. He is facing reality—death is inevitable and imminent. Later, when Stephen in Acts 7 is being crushed by huge stones thrown down on him, he said the same thing. It's clear that he also knows that death is inevitable and imminent. It's as if both Jesus and Stephen are saying, it's over, the end has come.

But when I continued reading the psalm and saw these words in context that is not what I saw. To be sure, the psalmist clearly is in trouble. He prays in verse 2, "Rescue me speedily," and in verse 4, "Take me out of the net that is hidden for me." Later in the psalm he cries out to God in distress, "My strength fails . . . , my bones waste away" (10). And he speaks of enemies who plot to take his life (13). In other verses, however, he thanks God for rescuing him. In fact, the entirety of verse 5 says, "Into your hand I commit my spirit; you have redeemed me, O Lord, faithful God." These are not the words of a man who thinks that life is over. Instead, he goes on to say, "I will exult and rejoice in your steadfast love because you have seen my affliction" (7). He may not be out of danger yet, but he has hope. In verses 14–15 he repeats and summarizes it for us: "I trust in you,

O Lord. I say, 'You are my God.' My times are in your hand" (Ps 31 NRSV). A cliché in the sports world says, "It's not over till it's over," and for the psalmist it is not over yet. The end has not come.

As I meditated on this psalm, I remembered that Jesus undoubtedly knew the entire psalm and understood exactly what the psalmist was saying. The fact that Jesus turned to it as he faced death means that these were not just his final words, they were his motto for life. "Into your hand I commit my spirit . . . my times are in your hand"—these words described how he lived as well as how he died. With such deep trust in God, Jesus knew that his life was not over and so he spoke the words of a psalm that faces the reality of pain, suffering, and death with faith, hope, and courage. In doing so he gave us a model for living that declares it's never over when God is in it with us. Therefore, the psalm ends with an exhortation for all of us: "Love the Lord, all you his saints. The Lord preserves the faithful . . . Be strong and let your heart take courage, all you who wait for the Lord" (Ps 31:24–25 NRSV).

As we take communion may this be our prayer also: "Father, into your hand I commit my spirit; my times are in your hands."

49

Perfection Required (and Made Possible) (GK)

People with perfect pitch flinch when they hear someone sing a little off-key. A perfectionist about appearance will let every stray hair make him or her feel uncomfortable. A skilled woodworker who is creating an intricate, inlaid pattern on a tabletop cannot tolerate even one slightly misaligned piece. An astronaut flying to the moon expects the math to be correct. A slight miscalculation would be disastrous.

If I were preparing a three-egg omelet for dinner I might think that one rotten egg out of three is okay, but I don't think my wife would find it acceptable. And yet, that is what we do with God. We bring him a life that is only a little bit out of tune, only slightly off course, only a little rotten, and we expect him to accept it. We humans tend to tolerate imperfection in the lives of others because that's all we get. We don't expect people to be perfect. We would have no fellowship at all if we insisted that everyone qualify by a life of perfection. But when it comes to being right with God perfection is required. Revelation 21 describes heaven, and verse 27 (NRSV) says clearly, "Nothing unclean will enter it." Perfection is required. What are we to do?

The Christians in Corinth faced this problem. Of all the churches seen in the New Testament the Corinthian church seemed to have more than its share of serious sinners. In 1 Corinthians 6 Paul acknowledges this. He lists some serious sins that they were guilty of, saying that those who do these things would not inherit the kingdom of God. But then he adds in verse 11, "and such were some of you. But you were washed, but you were sanctified, but you were justified in the name of the Lord Jesus and by the Spirit of our God" (1 Cor 6:11 NKJV).

We come to the Lord's Table as imperfect, unclean people made perfect and clean in Christ. Paul put it this way in 2 Corinthians 5:21 (NKJV), "For He made him who knew no sin to be sin for us, that we might become the righteousness of God in him." Let us partake, then, as people made righteous through that which is symbolized in the elements of communion, the bread which is his body, given for us, and the cup, which is the new covenant in his blood, shed for the remission of sin.

50

The Gruenewald Altarpiece (RH)

In the early 1990s when we were living and working in Tübingen, Germany, my wife and I made a trip to France. It takes a little more than two hours to drive from Tübingen to Strassburg, France. The drive takes you through the mountains of Germany's Black Forest. At Strassburg we turned south on the Rue de Vin, which is a highway running through the vineyards of northeastern France. We were headed for Colmar, a small city in France not far from the German border.

There was a famous Renaissance altarpiece on display in Colmar, painted by Mathias Gruenewald in the early sixteenth century, that I wanted to see. Today if you want to see it, you don't have to move to Germany, or book a flight to France. You can pull it up on WikiArt—though it's not quite the same experience! The work was originally done to stand in a monastery in Isenheim that focused on medical ministry treating people with skin diseases.

The central panel of this altarpiece depicts the crucifixion of Jesus. It's a gruesome picture showing Jesus' tortured body on the cross. In addition to the torturous wounds of crucifixion, the artist has covered Jesus' body with skin sores to emphasize his identification with the sufferings of humanity. To the right in the picture, as you face it, is the painting of a man who is supposed to be John the

Baptist. This, of course, is the artist taking liberty with history to make a point. John the Baptist was not present at the crucifixion of Jesus. Herod had beheaded him at least a year earlier. But in the picture John the Baptist is holding an open book in his left hand, probably representing the Old Testament Scriptures, since John the Baptist was considered to mark the end of the Hebrew prophets (see John 1:15–17) or, perhaps, more pointedly, it represents John the Baptist's words that "the law . . . was given through Moses, grace and truth came through Jesus Christ" (John 1:17 NRSV). With the index finger of his right hand John is pointing to Jesus and behind his right arm are John the Baptist's words, written in Latin, "He must increase but I must decrease" (John 3:30 NRSV). At John's feet stands a lamb looking up at Jesus on the cross. The lamb's right front leg is draped around a miniature cross that leans back on its shoulder, and under the lamb's neck stands a chalice with a stream of blood flowing from the lamb's neck into the chalice. One of the points I think the artist is making with the picture of the lamb is to suggest one of the first things that John says about Jesus when he first sees him, "Here is the lamb of God who takes away the sin of the world" (John 1:29 NRSV).

Gruenewald has captured the central points of the Lord's Supper in this center panel of his altarpiece. On the night that he was betrayed Jesus took bread, gave thanks, broke it, and said, This is my body given on your behalf. Do this to remember me. And he took a cup, and said, This cup is the new covenant in my blood which is poured out on your behalf.

51

Darkness over the Land (RH)

In Matthew 27:45 (NRSV), which is about the crucifixion of Jesus, it says: "From noon on darkness came over the whole land until three in the afternoon." And in John 1:29 (NRSV), we have the words of John the Baptist at the beginning of Jesus' ministry: "Here is the lamb of God who takes away the sin of the world."

In 2017 we witnessed a solar eclipse. In midmorning when it is normally bright with sunshine, we experienced darkness for a few minutes. My wife and I were living in western Oregon, which lay in the narrow path across the US where the eclipse was visible. It was something that will not occur again in our lifetimes. People were excited about the eclipse, and flocked to that part of the country to view it. My wife saw an aerial photo on the news of a line of traffic sixteen miles long creeping towards the small town of Prineville, Oregon. People paid enormous sums of money to rent rooms so they could be in the vicinity of the eclipse. Some religious leaders proclaimed that it was a sign from God. One pastor on the news said he saw it as a sign from God that people should repent. It wasn't. If people repented, that's good. I'm all for repentance. But the eclipse was something that God had programmed into the way the universe works when he created it. Solar eclipses have been occurring on a regular, predictable schedule for millennia, and people who study those kinds of things have been predicting them accurately for as far back as Western literature goes and probably longer.

Origen, who lived nearly 1,800 years ago, talks about solar eclipses in his commentary on the Gospel of Matthew. It is in his discussion of the darkness that shrouded the land for three hours when Jesus died on the cross (Matt 27:45). Origen says that some, who were antagonistic to the Christian faith, dismissed the reference to darkness on the land at Jesus' death as just an eclipse of the sun. Origen counters this argument by saying that an eclipse of the sun only occurs when the moon obstructs the rays of the sun. But, he adds, that this could not have happened when Christ was crucified because it was Passover time and Passover always occurred when the moon was full and reflected the full power of the sun at night. Both Origen and the opponents recognized that solar eclipses were regular, predictable occurrences that had been occurring for ages.[1]

That, of course, does not take away from the marvelous sight that we witnessed. But it was an indication of the amazing precision of God's creative power, not a special sign that he was sending at that particular moment in human history.

This brings me to John the Baptist's statement when he introduced Jesus to some of his disciples, "Here is the lamb of God who takes away the sin of the world" (John 1:29 NRSV). Origen, again, this time in his commentary on the Gospel of John, has something significant to say. He refers to the fact that there were numerous stories among both the Greeks and barbarian peoples about individuals who have intervened in some kind of major crisis, such as a plague or a famine, and had sacrificed themselves so that in some way the plague or famine might be averted. Then he says, "But never yet has a story been told of one who was able to take responsibility for purification on behalf of the whole world, that the whole world might be cleansed, since it would perish had he not taken responsibility to die on its behalf. Nor can such a story be told," Origen continues, "since Jesus alone has been able to take up into himself on the cross the burden of the sin of all on behalf of the whole world."[2]

<hr>

1. Origen, *Commentary on Matthew*, 745.

2. Origen, *Commentary on John: Books 13–32*, 325–26.

What we saw in the 2017 eclipse of the sun was an amazing sight. But it doesn't hold a candle to the event we gather at this table each week to celebrate when we partake of the bread and drink from the cup remembering Jesus' body and blood, broken and shed for the sins of all humanity, including our own.

52

Inextricably Entwined (GK)

I like the phrase "inextricably entwined." It's hard to say but its meaning is especially appropriate for Resurrection Sunday when we partake of the Lord's Supper. It means, of course, that certain things go together and simply cannot be separated. They are so interconnected that you cannot separate them without doing damage to each.

The cross and the resurrection are inextricably entwined. The cross, which is at the heart of the Lord's Supper, and the resurrection, which we celebrate on Easter, but also on the first day of every week, cannot be separated without doing damage to the meaning of each.

Take away the resurrection and what does that do to the meaning of the cross? It means Jesus died and remains dead like any other good man, like the prophets before him. He left behind some helpful teachings but, if he is still dead his teachings are like those of any other great person—inspirational but not redemptive. As Paul says in 1 Corinthians 15:17 (NRSV), "If Christ has not been raised, your faith is futile and you are still in your sins."

Take away the cross and what does that do to the meaning of the resurrection? There is nothing left to validate. It may be a marvelous miracle, but Jesus then is no different than Lazarus. He too was raised from the dead, but only for a time, and not to validate any redemptive or atoning sacrifice on his part. Jesus, on the other hand, came for the very purpose, as he put it, "to give his life a ransom for many" (Mark 10:45 NRSV).

In the upper room at the Last Supper Jesus held the bread and said, "This is my body, given for you," and the cup saying, "This is my blood . . . shed for the forgiveness of sins." Were these the rants of a self-deluded man? The empty tomb was a big exclamation mark that said NO! It is true. His death was not in vain. Paul put it all in one short sentence: "He was delivered over to death for our trespasses and was raised for our justification" (Rom 4:25 NRSV).

I wonder if some artistic person could come up with a piece of jewelry that would show the cross and the empty tomb inextricably entwined? We have lots of cross jewelry, but the cross without the resurrection is just an instrument of death—like a scaffold or an electric chair. Both the cross and the resurrection lose their power when separated.

How appropriate it is therefore, on Resurrection Sunday, that we remember the cross. Today we can give thanks that he was "delivered to death for our sins and raised for our justification."

53

Sponsored by Christ (GK)

I am sure that we are all familiar with the phrase "sponsored by"—you can fill in the rest: a stadium or team sponsored by a major corporation; a television program sponsored by a big company or, on public television, by a charitable foundation. In an earlier time kings would sponsor artists, singers, and poets. And we all know that "sponsored" means "paid for." I came across the story of a young German man who used the term in a unique way. It seems that his *oma (OH-ma),* German for Grandma, bought him his first car. It was a gift of love and a sacrifice for Oma to buy this car. In honor of her gift, to remember her gift, and so others would recognize the gift, he put a bumper sticker on his car that read "Sponsored bei Oma." In other words, "Paid for by Grandma."[1]

As Christians, maybe we should all wear a sign that says, "Sponsored by Christ." Paul said in 1 Corinthians 6:19–20 (NRSV), "Do you not know that . . . you are not your own? For you were bought with a price; therefore, glorify God in your body." There is an old Gospel hymn that says:

Redeemed, how I love to proclaim it!
Redeemed by the blood of the Lamb;
Redeemed thro' his infinite mercy,
his child, and forever I am.

1. Holloway, *Lest We Forget,* 65.

From the very beginning the church has been singing about being paid for by Christ. In Revelation 4 and 5 John describes a throne and the one who sat upon it who held a scroll that was sealed with seven seals. No one was found who was worthy to open the book and John began to weep greatly. One of the twenty-four elders told him to stop weeping because the Lion from the tribe of Judah, the Root of David has overcome and he can open it. Then John looked, and perhaps expected to see a ferocious lion, but instead he saw a lamb standing as if slain, who came and took the book out of the right hand of him who sat upon the throne. At this the four living creatures, representing the animal and human world, and the twenty-four elders, representing all of the church, sang a new song:

> You are worthy to take the scroll and to open its seals,
> for you were slaughtered and by your blood you ran-
> somed for God
> saints from every tribe and language and people and
> nation;
> you have made them to be a kingdom and priests serving
> our God,
> and they will reign on the earth (Rev 5:9–10 NRSV).

When we come to the table, we remember that this is our song, our story, our claim as well. We are all "sponsored by Christ," paid for by him.

54

About Being Solvent (GK)

May I ask a rather impertinent question? Are you solvent? A lot of businesses, families, and even governments today are not solvent, although I am sure they all want to be. The first meaning of the term is that one can pay all legal debts, and we all want that.

I began thinking about this word when I read a meditation on Psalm 38 and was struck by the author's statement: "*Sin is the great solvent of our relationships.*"[1] My use of the term just now and this author's are quite different. My curiosity about the difference led me to the dictionary, where I discovered two meanings which appear to be unrelated. One is the ability to pay debts. The other says that a solvent is a substance that dissolves another substance. How can these definitions be related?

This question brought me back to Psalm 38, where David sadly confesses that his sin had separated him from his family and from his God. Sin, like a great solvent, dissolves and destroys relationships. I remember that several years ago, my wife, using a mercury-filled thermometer, accidently broke it and the mercury rolled out across her fingers, contacted her gold wedding ring, and dissolved what it touched. That is what sin does to our relationships. It destroys that which is valuable and precious—our relationships with spouse, children, or friends.

1. Reardon, *Christ,* 74.

But there is a positive side to a solvent. In many cases, it cleanses in the act of dissolving. Whether it is paint in a brush or tar on your car, a good solvent will remove it. And so it is with our sin. A good solvent will dissolve the sin and cleanse us. Thus, we read in 1 John 1:7 (NKJV), "If we walk in the light as he is in the light . . . the blood of Jesus Christ, His son, cleanses us from all sin." These words remind us that Jesus said at the Last Supper, *This cup is the new covenant in my blood, which is shed for you* (Luke 22:20 NKJV).

Now I know the connection between the two definitions of the word "solvent." Our debts have been dissolved and removed through the sacrifice of Christ. We are right with God again. In his eyes we are solvent, all debts paid, because of the sin-cleansing blood of Christ.

55

Christ the Gambler (RH)

In Matthew's account of the crucifixion of Jesus, after the victims were all lifted up on their crosses, he says, "And when they had crucified him, they divided his clothes among themselves by casting lots; then they sat down there and kept watch over him" (Matt 27:35–36 NRSV). A British poet and chaplain in World War I named G. A. Studdert Kennedy wrote a poem about the far greater gamble going on at the crucifixion of Jesus than that taking place among the soldiers who were throwing dice for Jesus' clothing. Kennedy gave his poem the title "He Was a Gambler Too," and says in it:

> There while they played with dice,
> He made His Sacrifice,
> And died upon the Cross to rid
> God's world of sin.

The crucifixion was a great gamble for Jesus. Could he endure it? We tend to think of the events in the life of Jesus as cut and dried. He did this, knowing that such and such was going to happen, so he took no great risk. But all of the Gospels insist that he was human. That means, among other things, that he was limited in what he knew. When Paul later reflected on this he referred to Christ *emptying himself* of his divinity and taking the form of a slave and dying a slave's death on a cross (Phil 2:6–8). I think the one thing Jesus was sure of as he approached that fateful Passover day was that the end of his life was very near and that it was going to be a very painful end. Before his arrest in the garden, Matthew says Jesus went forward alone, beyond his disciples, and "threw himself on the ground and prayed, 'My Father, if it is possible, let this cup pass from me; yet not what I want but what you want'" (Matt 26:39 NRSV). He did this three times, praying the same prayer. I suspect this is what the author of Hebrews is alluding to when he says, "In the days of his flesh, Jesus offered up prayers and supplications, with loud cries and tears, to the one who was able to save him from death" (Heb 5:7 NRSV). And then there was that prayer on the cross when Jesus cried out in the words of the Twenty-Second Psalm, "My God, my God, why have you forsaken me?" (Mark 15:34 NRSV). Studdert Kennedy concludes his poem with the words,

> He took his life and threw
> It for a world redeemed.
> And eer the westering sun went down,
> Crowning that day with its crimson crown,
> He knew that He had won.[1]

The soldiers with the military power of Rome behind them; the priestly hierarchy in Jerusalem with its fears, accusations, and secret plots against Jesus, had lost. Easter was just two days away. And *then* the soldiers were trembling and frozen with fear; the priestly hierarchy in Jerusalem was shaken with confusion. Jesus had redeemed God's world from sin! We gather at this table to celebrate that victory, and not just on Easter Sunday, but every Sunday, because in a sense, every Sunday is a commemoration of the death and resurrection of Jesus.

1. Kennedy, *Unutterable Beauty*, 104.

56

The Cost of Compassion (GK)

How much does it cost to love and be compassionate? Two passages by John, both with the reference 3:16, one in the Gospel and the other in his first epistle, portray the cost of compassion. First John 3:16 says, "We know love by this, that he laid down his life for us; and we ought to lay down our lives for the brethren" (NRSV).

Henri Nouwen wrote about how he learned a valuable lesson about love and compassion when he was thirteen years old. It was during the last year of World War II and his father had given him a little goat to care for. They lived in a part of Holland that was isolated by great rivers from the D-day armies. But people were dying from hunger. Nouwen said:

> I loved my little goat. I spent hours collecting acorns for him, taking him on long walks, and playfully fighting with him, pushing him where his two horns were growing. I carried him in my arms, built a pen for him in the garage, and gave him a little wooden wagon to pull. Walter and I were best friends. One day, early in the morning when I entered the garage, I found the pen empty. Walter had been stolen. I don't remember ever having cried so vehemently and so long. I sobbed and screamed from grief. My father and mother hardly knew how to console me. It was the first time that I learned about love and loss.

He continued, "Years later, when the war was over and we had enough food again, my father told me that our gardener had taken Walter and fed him to his family who had nothing left to eat. My father knew it was the gardener, but he never confronted him— even though he saw my grief. I now realize that both Walter and my father taught me something about compassion."[1]

When people are dying it often costs a great deal to save them. In this case it meant the loss of Nouwen's pet goat. It also cost the father a great deal to see his son suffer so much. While not an exact parallel, it says something about our heavenly Father's love and compassion and what it cost him. To see that cost we need only look at the cross. There we see the love and compassion of God who gave his Son for our salvation.

How much does it cost to be compassionate? In God's case, it cost the death of his Son. Each Sunday as we come to the Lord's Table it should remind us of John 3:16 (NKJV), "For God so loved the world that he gave his only begotten son . . ." In the bread and in the cup, we see also the love and compassion of the Son who paid the ultimate price to rescue us from death.

1. Nouwen, *Here and Now*, 48.

57

Visible Signs of the Resurrection (GK)

He is risen! (*He* is risen indeed!) But how do we know?

Many visual testimonies to the resurrection of Christ can be seen in the Gospels. Among them are the stone rolled away, the empty tomb, and one of the most intriguing, the abandoned grave clothes. John 20:6–7 (NRSV) tells us that when Peter and John ran to investigate the empty tomb, they "saw the linen wrappings lying there, and the cloth that had been on Jesus' head, not lying with the linen wrappings, but rolled up in a place by itself." As though he had just stepped out of them, the linen cloths were just lying there. The headcloth, carefully folded or rolled up, was some distance away.

On the internet you will find that some are saying that his folded handkerchief, or towel, or as the King James version says, "napkin," points to a Jewish custom. If the master leaves a meal unfinished and wads up his napkin and throws it down, it means he is finished. But if he carefully folds it and lays it on the table it says to his servant, "I am not finished—I will be back." Could this be what the folded headcloth means? Perhaps, although research indicates that there is no proof that this was the custom in Jewish households, and we might question the idea that a dinner napkin was used as a grave headcloth. This much is certain, the abandoned grave cloths and the carefully folded headcloth say that the body was not stolen by a fast-moving body snatcher. Rather, they point to the calm, unhurried exit by one who had no further need of them.

There is another visible testimony to the resurrection that outweighs all others, the weekly gathering of disciples to commune with their living Lord. If Jesus was still in the tomb, and had never shown himself to his disciples, there is no way that a few disciples could resurrect their fellowship. They could not have fooled themselves and others and pulled off the greatest hoax ever seen. They knew in their hearts, deep down, that he was alive, and they were willing to do whatever it took to meet with him weekly at his table. The very existence of the church is a result of the resurrection and its most powerful witness.

At the table, then, we proclaim not only the Lord's death but also his resurrection. It is the resurrection that created our community of faith and hope. We, as the church and as individuals, have, as Peter said, "been born again to a living hope through the resurrection of Jesus Christ from the dead" (1 Pet 1:3 NAS).

58

When Jesus Leaves, What Then? (GK)

How would you feel and what would you do if you suddenly lost the most influential person in your life? Suppose there was someone who was so strong and yet filled with love, so compassionate and yet convicting, so powerful and yet vulnerable that you felt you could not live without that person, and suddenly he/she is gone. How would you feel? What would you do?

According to Luke's Gospel this happened to two men after Jesus was crucified. As they made their way from Jerusalem to Emmaus, heartbroken because their Lord had died, Jesus suddenly came to them, but they did not recognize him. Finally, as he ate with them, when he blessed and broke the bread, their eyes were opened and they recognized him.

Luke continues by saying that Jesus then vanished from their sight. Immediately they hurried back to Jerusalem and told the eleven apostles and others how they recognized Jesus "in the breaking of the bread." Luke continues, "While they were telling these things, He himself stood in their midst and said to them, 'Peace be to you'" (Luke 24:36 NAS). We can understand when Luke says that they were startled and frightened.

Jesus urged them not to be afraid, to look at him, touch him, see that he had flesh and bones, and they were not seeing a ghost.

Here he is in his resurrected body, a body appropriate to the environment. So much so that he can ask, "Have you anything here to eat?" They gave him a piece of broiled fish and he ate it before them.

Then Jesus began to teach them, as he had the two disciples earlier on the road to Emmaus. Luke says, "He opened their minds to understand the scriptures," telling them that the Messiah would suffer and rise again from the dead, and that "repentance and forgiveness of sins" would be "proclaimed in his name to all the nations, beginning from Jerusalem. You are witnesses of these things. And see, I am sending upon you what my Father promised" and you will be "clothed with power from on high" (Luke 24:45–49 NRSV).

After the teaching he led them out of Jerusalem as far as Bethany, where he was carried away into heaven. Jesus was gone. This man who had changed their lives, who opened their minds to God's word, who loved them with sacrificial love—he was gone.

You might expect Luke to describe how sad they felt, but he doesn't. His final words are these: "And they worshiped him and returned to Jerusalem with great joy; and they were continually in the temple blessing God" (Luke 24:52–53 NRSV).

Ever since, even though his resurrected body left this earth and we cannot see him, we know that we will experience his presence in the breaking of the bread, and thus, like the early disciples, we continue to worship and then go out with joyful praise to be his witnesses.

59

Pentecost and the Gift of the Spirit (RH)

Isn't it great that we do not have to understand things completely before we can use them and enjoy their benefits? It would be awful to have to understand everything about electricity before we could turn on an electric light, or have any electric appliances. I won't even suggest the use of computers! There are many things whose fruits I enjoy but whose nature and manner of working I do not understand. I don't fully understand how plants grow, but I know how to till the soil and plant seeds, and can, therefore, enjoy the fresh produce of a garden.

The Bible tells us that God has given the Christian his Spirit. In John 16 Jesus promised to send the Spirit after his return to the Father. The disciples experienced that sending on the day of Pentecost when they were gathered in Jerusalem. Pentecost Sunday is the day on which the church traditionally remembers that outpouring of the Holy Spirit that is described in Acts 2. There were many things accompanying it that no one present fully understood. But one thing was very clear. God had given a new power to the followers of Jesus.

We may be thankful that it is not necessary to understand everything about the Holy Spirit in order to enjoy the benefits. Our lives as Christians would be impoverished if we lacked the benefits of the Spirit. Paul provides a list of some of those benefits in Romans 8. He says the Spirit sets us free from the law of sin and death (8:2) and gives us peace of mind (8:5–8). The Spirit assures our future resurrection (8:11, 23–5), and makes us heirs of God (8:14–17). Finally Paul says that the Spirit helps us in our weakness (8:26), and helps us pray (8:26–7).

I call your attention to just one of those benefits. Paul says the Spirit assures our future resurrection. I once heard Halford Luccock, who was a professor of preaching at Yale University in the mid-twentieth century, tell the story of a man who had visited a small village in Maine that was to be flooded by a large lake that was built for a hydroelectric plant. Once the people in the village knew that their village was to be destroyed, everything began to deteriorate. No houses were painted, no roofs repaired, no potholes in the streets filled. The man telling the story commented, "Where there is no faith in the future, there is no power in the present." The Spirit given by God brings us hope for the future. In 2 Corinthians 1:22 Paul speaks of the Spirit as the deposit, or down payment, God has given us. The New International Version has added an interpretive phrase to that verse, which catches the idea of the deposit when it says that this guarantees "what is to come."

That promise of resurrection, that future hope, is actually present in the words of Jesus in Matthew's Gospel that he speaks over the bread and wine the night of his arrest. "While they were eating, Jesus took a loaf of bread, and after blessing it he broke it, gave it to the disciples, and said, 'Take, eat; this is my body.' Then he took a cup, and after giving thanks he gave it to them, saying, 'Drink from it, all of you; for this is my blood of the covenant, which is poured out for many for the forgiveness of sins. I tell you, I will never again drink of this fruit of the vine *until that day when I drink it new with you in my Father's kingdom*'" (Matt 26:26–29 NRSV, my emphasis). There is the promise for the future that gives the Christian power day by day. The Spirit that we have received is the guarantee for that promise that lies in our futures. When we partake of the Lord's Supper we are anticipating that day in our future when we will be united with our Lord in the Father's kingdom.

60

Pentecost and the Power of the Spirit (RH)

In the second chapter of Acts it says, "When the day of Pentecost had come, they were all together in one place. And suddenly from heaven there came a sound like the rush of a violent wind, and it filled the entire house where they were sitting. Divided tongues, as of fire, appeared among them, and a tongue rested on each of them. All of them were filled with the Holy Spirit and began to speak in other languages, as the Spirit gave them ability" (Acts 2:1–4 NRSV).

Today is Pentecost Sunday. It is the day the church celebrates the outpouring of the Holy Spirit, fifty days after the resurrection of Jesus. The story in Acts 2 is the only place in the Bible the event is recorded. The story was written up and preserved by the evangelist Luke, who also wrote the Gospel of Luke. Those verses in Acts 2 link the ministry of the church with the ministry of Jesus. In his Gospel Luke shows that the ministry of Jesus was inaugurated by the outpouring of the Holy Spirit on Jesus at his baptism (Luke 3:21–22). Luke also says that Jesus began his ministry "filled with the power of the Spirit" (Luke 4:14–15 NRSV).

But it is not just the beginning of Jesus' ministry; it is his entire ministry that takes places in "the power of the Spirit." Luke places Jesus' whole ministry under the words of Isaiah 61:1–2, which begins by saying, "The Spirit of the Lord is upon me" (Luke 4:17–19

NRSV). At the close of Luke's Gospel Jesus instructs his disciples to wait in Jerusalem until he sends the "power from on high" to be with them (Luke 24:49 NRSV). And, now, in Acts 2, as that group of believers in Jesus who have been waiting in Jerusalem and who will later be referred to as the church, begins to carry on Jesus' ministry, Luke records the coming of that "power from on high" and shows that the ministry of the church, like the ministry of Jesus himself, is performed in the power of the Spirit of God.

But the church is sometimes uneasy about the subject of the Holy Spirit. The tradition in which I stand is a bit uneasy about the Holy Spirit. I have been in this tradition my entire life and have participated in churches in this tradition in several states in the US and other parts of the world, and these churches tend not to talk much about the Holy Spirit.

There is a lot of mystery about the Spirit. After all, that scene that I read described in Acts 2 is not your normal Sunday morning worship service! There was fire from heaven, and noise, and confusion, and eleven men from Galilee speaking other languages. But the thing that many people find most disturbing about the Holy Spirit is what is referred to as the gifts of the Spirit. Most people, who know anything about the Holy Spirit, know the texts in 1 Corinthians 12–14 where Paul discusses gifts such as speaking in tongues, prophesying, and healing. And because many are also aware of fraudulent claims made for some of these gifts—in ancient times, just as today—they are hesitant to say much about the Spirit.

But there is another list of gifts of the Spirit, also written by Paul, in Romans 12:6–8 (NRSV): "We have gifts that differ according to the grace given to us," and then he lists the gifts with instructions on how they should be put to use: "prophecy, in proportion to faith; ministry, in ministering; the teacher, in teaching; the exhorter, in exhortation; the giver, in generosity; the leader, in diligence; the compassionate, in cheerfulness." That is a less disturbing list of gifts for most people.

What does the outpouring of the Holy Spirit have to do with this act that we perform each Sunday and call by various names, one of which is communion, or sharing? Everything! It is the work of the Spirit that we remember Jesus of Nazareth. It is the work of the Spirit that we continue to carry on the ministry that Jesus performed—the ministry of proclaiming forgiveness of sins, the ministry of helping the poor and serving the sick, the ministry of announcing the coming day of the Lord. The work of the church is ministry in the power of the Spirit.

Bibliography

The Apostolic Fathers: Greek Texts and English Translations. 3rd ed. Edited and translated by Michael W. Holmes. Grand Rapids: Baker Academic, 2007.

Augustine. *On Christian Doctrine.* Translated by D. W. Robertson Jr. Indianapolis: Bobbs Merrill, 1958.

Craddock, Fred. *Luke.* Louisville: John Knox, 1990.

Cullmann, Oscar, and F. J. Leenhardt. *Essays on the Lord's Supper.* Richmond, VA: John Knox, 1958.

Hammarskjold, Dag. *Markings.* New York: Vintage, 2006.

Hays, Richard B. *First Corinthians.* Louisville: John Knox, 1997.

Holloway, Clinton J. *Lest We Forget.* Nashville: Cold Tree, 2008.

Kennedy, G. A. Studdert. *The Unutterable Beauty.* London: Hodder and Stoughton, 1964.

Killinger, John. *Fundamentals of Preaching.* Minneapolis: Fortress, 1996.

Migne, J. P., ed. *Patrologiae Graecae* 28. Turnholt: Brepols, 1857.

Moltmann, Jürgen. *The Living God and the Fullness of Life.* Translated by Margaret Kohl. Louisville: Westminster John Knox, 2015.

Morse, Gertrude. *The Dogs May Bark but the Caravan Moves On.* Joplin, MO: College, 1999.

The New Interpreter's Study Bible: New Revised Standard Version with the Apocrypha. Nashville: Abingdon, 2003.

Nouwen, Henri. *Can You Drink the Cup?* Notre Dame, IN: Ave Maria, 2012.

———. *Here and Now: Living in the Spirit.* New York: Crossroad, 1994.

Origen. *Commentary on the Gospel according to John: Books 1–10.* FOTC 80. Translated by Ronald E. Heine. Washington, DC: The Catholic University of America, 1989.

———. *Commentary on the Gospel according to John: Books 13–32.* FOTC 89. Translated by Ronald E. Heine. Washington, DC: The Catholic University of America, 1993.

———. *The Commentary of Origen on the Gospel of St Matthew.* Vol. 2. Translated by Ronald E. Heine. Oxford: Oxford University Press, 2018.

———. *Homilies on Genesis and Exodus*. Translated by Ronald E. Heine. FOTC 71. Washington, DC: The Catholic University of America, 1982.

Patterson, Ben. *God's Prayer Book*. Carol Stream, IL: Saltriver, 2008.

Reardon, Patrick. *Christ in the Psalms*. Ben Lomond, CA: Conciliar, 2000.

Remen, Rachel Naomi. *My Grandfather's Blessings: Stories of Strength, Refuge, and Belonging*. New York: Riverhead, 2000.

Richardson, Alan. *An Introduction to the Theology of the New Testament*. London: SCM, 1958.

Rienecker, Fritz. *A Linguistic Key to the Greek New Testament*. Grand Rapids: Zondervan, 1980.

Thielicke, Helmut. *Christ and the Meaning of Life*. Edited and translated by John W. Doberstein. New York: Harper and Row, 1962.

Wiesel, Elie. *The Gates of the Forest*. Translated by Frances Frenays. New York: Avon, 1967.

Witherington, Ben, III. *Making a Meal of It*. Waco, TX: Baylor University Press, 2007.

Wright, N. T. *John for Everyone Part 1: Chapters 1–10*. Louisville: Westminster John Knox, 2004.

———. *The Meal Jesus Gave Us*. Louisville: Westminster John Knox, 1999.

Zahnd, Brian. *Beauty Will Save the World*. Lake Mary, FL: Charisma House, 2012.